SWATZPROJECTZ TRAVEL GUIDE

TO

TROGIR

CROATIA

Insider Guide to Trogir's Best-Kept Secrets

Orson Noel

COPYRIGHT NOTICE

DISCLAIMER

Please note that the information contained within this document is for educational purposes only. The information contained herein has been obtained from sources believed to be reliable at the time of publication. The opinions expressed herein are subject to change without notice.

Readers acknowledge that the Author / Publisher is not engaging in rendering legal, financial or professional advice. The Publisher / Author disclaims all warranties as to the accuracy, completeness, or adequacy of such information.

The Publisher assumes no liability for errors, omissions, or inadequacies in the information contained herein or from the interpretations thereof. The publisher / Author specifically disclaims any liability from the use or application of the information contained herein or from the interpretations thereof.

TABLE OF CONTENT

INTRODUCTION

WELCOME TO TROGIR.

Ah, Trogir! Just hearing the name makes me smile and brings back sun-soaked memories. I've seen several medieval towns in my travels, but there's something special about this small island-city, a place so well kept that it feels like you've stepped straight onto a movie set - only this is genuine, vibrant, and totally lovely. Trogir is known as "The Museum City," and the term is well-deserved. But instead of stuffy halls and glass exhibits, imagine an entire town as a living, breathing museum, with every stone, alleyway, and sun-dappled piazza telling a millennia-long narrative.

I discovered Trogir years ago, almost by accident, while driving along the Dalmatian coast. I was on my way to Split when I noticed a little signpost. Curiosity, as it frequently does for us travelers, got the best of me. I was hooked from the minute I crossed the first small bridge onto the island. It wasn't only the spectacular Romanesque-Gothic architecture or the dazzling Adriatic seas lapping at its ancient foundations; it was the place's whole atmosphere. It felt as if time had stopped here, enabling the greatest of its history to crystallize.

WHY TROGIR? A GLIMPSE OF ITS TIMELESS CHARM

So, why Trogir? What distinguishes this location from the many other stunning locations along Croatia's coastline? For me, it's the overwhelming amount of beauty and history crammed into such a little place. The whole Old Town is a UNESCO World Heritage site, and you'll understand why within minutes of arrival. It is a masterwork of human creation, with Greek, Roman, and Venetian elements perfectly blending over ages to create a harmonic architectural symphony.

Imagine walking through small, polished-stone pathways, the sunshine trickling down to reveal the delicate intricacies of a centuries-old sculpture over a doorway. You'll pass majestic mansions erected by wealthy Venetian families, with windows still facing out into the busy Riva (promenade). You'll find little chapels tucked away in peaceful nooks and emerge onto squares dominated by spectacular monuments like as the Cathedral of St. Lawrence, which has Radovan's Portal, a piece of art so intricate you may spend an hour admiring it.

But Trogir is more than its stones. It's the scent of sea air combined with freshly made bread from a local pekara. It's the sound of klapa singers practicing in a secret courtyard, their harmonies reverberating off the old walls. It's the sight of local fisherman repairing their nets on the shoreline, their cheeks tanned by the sun and sea. It's the flavor of fresh grilled fish coated with local olive oil, eaten at a waterfront konoba while the sky becomes a blazing orange. This isn't a ghost town; it's a vibrant, alive community where everyday life unfolds against an incredible setting. Trogir's seductive, eternal beauty stems from its unique combination of the colossal and the banal, the ancient and ordinary.

TROGIR FOR FIRST-TIMERS: WHAT TO EXPECT

If this is your first time dancing with Trogir, be prepared to be completely enchanted. My first piece of advice? Wear comfy shoes! The Old Town is a pedestrian paradise, and you'll have a lot of fun exploring. As you cross the bridge from the mainland, you'll notice a slight shift: you've entered a different universe. Expect to become deliciously lost in its convoluted passageways; that is half the enjoyment. Each turn exposes a different view, a secret patio, or a nice café.

The Old Town itself is small, so you won't be overwhelmed by distances, but you'll be surprised at how much history is crammed in. The stately Kamerlengo Fortress stands watch at the water's edge, providing stunning panoramic views. You'll walk down the Riva, which is dotted with palm trees, cafés, and glittering yachts; it's Trogir's social hub, and it's alive with activity, especially on sunny evenings.

Expect a magnificent assault on your senses: sparkling white stone, beautiful blue Adriatic waters, and vibrant bougainvillea bursting over historic walls. You'll hear talks in Croatian, Italian, and a dozen other languages, waves lapping gently, and the odd church bell tolling the hour. Experience the best of Dalmatian cuisine with fresh fish, pašticada (slow-cooked beef stew), and exquisite local wines.

Beyond the Old Town, the island of Čiovo, accessed by another bridge, offers a distinct ambiance, with beaches, coves, and more contemporary amenities, offering a wonderful balance to the historical core. Essentially, first-timers may expect to fall in love. Trogir has a knack of grabbing hearts swiftly and easily.

Trogir for Returning Visitors: Discovering New Layers

Welcome back! If you're returning to Trogir, you've already experienced its charm. You undoubtedly have your favorite locations - that small café with the perfect macchiato, that seat on the Riva where you like watching the world go by, or that alleyway that always makes you grab for your camera. But let me tell you that Trogir always has more mysteries to reveal and layers to unravel. I find that with each visit, I learn something new or experience a familiar site through new eyes.

Perhaps this time you'll explore further away from the regular tourist routes. Perhaps you'll explore the calmer northern part of the Old Town, which has hidden residential courtyards. Explore Čiovo's hidden coves and hiking paths for breathtaking vistas of the Old Town. Have you ever taken a local cooking lesson or spent the afternoon sampling olive oils with a local producer?

This guide is also built with you in mind. Look for the "Hidden Gems" areas, or take one of the "Day Trips" to explore the surrounding area. Perhaps you'll come in a different season - Trogir in the spring, with wildflowers blossoming, or in the mellow fall, offers an entirely different, more calm experience than the summer hustle. Returning tourists describe Trogir as being like visiting an old friend: familiar and reassuring, but always having fresh tales to tell and experiences to share.

How to Use This Guide

I've put my experiences and passion for Trogir onto these pages, intending to create a resource that is both inspiring and extremely useful. Consider me a well-traveled acquaintance who can give you the inside scoop. This guide is designed to help you organize your vacation, whether you're a diligent planner or a more spontaneous individual.

We'll start with the basics: learning about Trogir's history and layout, practical pre-trip planning, and how to traverse the town. Then we get into the core of the experience: the famous landmarks that you can't miss, as well as the lovely hidden jewels that I've found over the years. We'll choose the ideal place to stay, from budget-friendly options to deluxe retreats, as well as explore exciting activities and indulge in a gourmet tour of Trogir's greatest restaurants.

You'll discover sections on shopping, eco-tourism (since we all want to travel sustainably), amazing day excursions, and even crafted itineraries for various sorts of travelers and durations of stay. And, of course, I've included the essential "Do's and Don'ts" as well as a helpful list of basic Croatian words to help you interact with the amazing locals.

Feel free to skip to the areas that interest you the most. Use the itineraries as a starting point, then tailor them to your own speed and interests. The Appendix at the rear is full with useful addresses and contact information to make your travel easier.

Finally, I hope that this guide will inspire you to plan your ideal Trogir journey, full of exploration, joy, and wonderful experiences. So, flip the page and let us explore Trogir's ageless beauty together. Your journey awaits!

CHAPTER 1

UNDERSTANDING TROGIR'S HISTORY, CULTURE, AND PEOPLE

Before you decide which beach to visit or what exquisite seafood to order, let us first get to know this town's spirit. It's like meeting a fascinating person: you want to learn about their past, passions, what makes them laugh, and what they value. Trogir is no different.

A STORIED PAST: FROM TRAGURION TO THE UNESCO WORLD HERITAGE

Imagine we're inside a time machine. Our first stop? Way back in the third century BCE. It was here when Greek immigrants, brave explorers from the island of Issa (now Vis), inspected this small island and said, "Yep, this is the spot." They called it Tragurion, which is sometimes translated as "goat island." Despite its unappealing name, this little island was strategically located between the mainland and the bigger island of Čiovo, providing protection from both sides. They actually built the town we know today.

The Romans then arrived, as they do in so many parts of the world. They were skilled builders, and Trogir thrived under their dominion, becoming a prominent port. However, the true architectural enchantment, the style that marks Trogir's gorgeous old town, arrived later with the Venetians. The Venetian Republic ruled Trogir for about four centuries, from the early 1400s until the late 1700s. Oh, did they make their mark! The beautiful palaces with their intricate balconies, the wide loggias where public life unfolded, and the massive Kamerlengo Fortress guarding the sea - so much of this fine masonry speaks of Venetian talent and influence. It resembles a little Venice, but with a unique Dalmatian heart.

Of course, history did not end there. The Austrians arrived, followed by a brief period under Napoleon's French Empire (which left behind the fairly attractive Marmont's Gloriette), and then back to the Austrians, until Trogir became a part of Yugoslavia. Despite all of these swings and transformations, through sieges and celebrations, Trogir somehow retained its medieval essence. The street pattern established down centuries ago remains the one you'll follow now. Buildings from its golden heyday still stand proudly.

This amazing preservation, this nearly totally intact ancient urban setting, won Trogir a distinguished spot on the UNESCO World Heritage list in 1997. When you go through those gates, you enter a living museum, where each cobblestone has a tale to tell. It's not only ancient; it's timeless.

THE SOUL OF DALMATIA: TROGIR'S UNIQUE CULTURAL IDENTITY.

Now, Trogir is indisputably Dalmatian. You'll feel the legendary Dalmatian spirit in the air, a wonderful mix of gentle charm (fjaka, that delightful state of joyous indolence, is a real thing here!), fierce pride in their cultural heritage, a deep connection to the gleaming Adriatic, and a profound love for life's simple pleasures: fresh food, good local wine, and the warmth of community.

Trogir, however, has a distinct shine within the larger Dalmatian identity. What actually distinguishes it for me is its extraordinary artistic heritage. We're talking about world-class goods. Consider the Cathedral of St. Lawrence, for example. Its main entrance, Radovan's Portal, carved in 1240, is more than just a gateway; it is a masterwork of

Romanesque-Gothic sculpture, so complex and alive that it will take your breath away. I've stood in front of it lots of times, and every time I spot something new. Then there's the famed Kairos relief, a fine Greek sculpture from the third century BC discovered just here in Trogir. It represents Kairos, the deity of the appropriate time, a transitory figure you must grab by the forelock before he vanishes. It's become a symbol of the town, a wonderful reminder to live in the moment, something Trogir appears to have perfected.

The marine tradition is also strongly ingrained in Trogir's psyche. For centuries, it was an important harbor, a hub for shipbuilding and commerce. That link to the sea can still be felt in the subtle creak of fishing boats, the salty aroma borne by the breeze, and the lingering stories of sailors. Unlike some of the bigger seaside cities, Trogir's old town maintains an intimate, almost village-like ambiance, even when the summer throngs are at their peak. Trogir's distinct cultural stamp stems from this strong combination of significant creative tradition, deep historical roots, and a wonderfully maintained, human-scale town. The Trogirani, the locals, hold their heritage with quiet pride, which is a delight to see.

Local Culture and Traditions: Festivals, Customs, and Community

While the old stones tell stories of monarchs and artists, Trogir is very much alive, pulsing with the rhythms of daily life and long-held customs. To properly connect with the town, you must understand its rhythms.

One of the first places you'll notice this is the Riva, the magnificent palm-fringed promenade that serves as the town's social hub. From early morning, when locals meet for their first strong coffee of the day, to the evening korzo (the typical leisurely promenade), the Riva is where Trogir goes to see and be seen, to converse, laugh, and just enjoy the breathtaking views. My advice? Do what the locals do. Find a café, order a drink, and simply watch the world go by. It's a lesson in pomalo, the great Dalmatian notion of slowing down and enjoying the present moment.

Don't miss the Pazar, a busy open-air market located just across the river on the mainland. It's an experience for the senses! Heaps of sun-ripened fruits and vegetables, fragrant local cheeses, golden olive oils, jars of rich honey, and bunches of fragrance lavender - it's the ideal spot to enjoy local delicacies and maybe purchase a real, non-touristy memento.

Trogir glows all year with festivals and activities that highlight its unique culture. The Trogir Cultural Summer, which brings music, folklore performances, and open-air theater to the town's old squares and courtyards, adds to the charm of summer. If you get the opportunity to hear klapa singing - that hauntingly beautiful traditional Dalmatian acapella harmony - reverberating across a stone courtyard on a warm night, I guarantee it will give you shivers. Religious festivals, like as the feast day of St. Lawrence (Sveti Lovro) in August, are also significant communal events, with processions and firmly held customs. Family and community are fundamental here. You'll witness generations eating together and children playing freely in the squares; it's a pleasant reminder of what actually counts.

THE TROGIR VIBE: WHAT MAKES IT UNIQUE

So how does Trogir feel? If I were to sum up its essence, I'd describe it as a compelling combination of old grandeur and intimate charm, with a splash of coastal romance. There is an almost physical sense of history surrounding you, yet it is not like being in a stuffy museum. It is alive. It breathes. It encourages you to take part in its continuous tale.

During the day, particularly during peak season, the old town is alive with an infectious vitality. Visitors from all around the world will speak in a variety of languages as they discover its delights. However, when the afternoon sun sinks lower, spreading lengthy shadows and bathing the honey-colored stone in a warm, ethereal glow, a new type of magic descends. The passageways get quieter and more ominous. The gentle lights from bustling konobas (traditional pubs) stream out into the piazzas, enticing visitors to linger. The air cools, transporting the saline tang of the Adriatic and the delectable perfume of grilled fish. It's really romantic, the type of environment that makes you want to grasp someone's hand and stroll.

Trogir is particularly unusual in that it strikes a magnificent balance between its towering heritage and its extremely human scale. The cathedral's majestic bell tower, a tribute to centuries of devotion and creativity, can take your breath away in one moment. The next, you may sneak down a short, winding corridor barely big enough to stretch your arms, only to find yourself in a little, sun-dappled courtyard with a local family having a meal and washing draped carelessly between antique walls. This dynamic interaction - the grandeur of history and the simple beauty of everyday living, the eternal stone and the ever-present sea - is what makes Trogir so unique.

Wrapping Up

It does more than simply dazzle you with its beauty; it draws you, welcomes you, and finds a place in your heart to remain long after you've sailed away. And there, my friends, is the Trogir vibe: completely memorable.

CHAPTER 2

TROGIR'S KEY NEIGHBORHOODS AND LAYOUT.

One of the first things you'll notice about Trogir is its distinctive geography. It's not just one landmass; it's a fascinating puzzle of islands, mainlands, and bridges that connect them. Let's break it down so you can navigate like a local (or at least a highly knowledgeable guest!).

OLD TOWN (GRAD): AN ISLAND OF HISTORY

This, my friends, is the heart and soul of Trogir, the "Museum City". The Old Town, also known as Grad by locals, is located on a small island between the Croatian mainland and the larger island of Čiovo. Two bridges serve as your gateways: one connects you to the mainland and the other, a newer one, leads you to Čiovo. This island setting gives the Old Town an incredibly contained and historic feel.

No cars are permitted within its ancient walls, which is a complete blessing.

Navigation of the Labyrinthine Streets

Now when I say "labyrinthine," I really mean it! The streets here are beautiful, confusing maze of narrow, polished limestone alleyways. They curve and turn, open into small squares, and sometimes appear to lead nowhere before surprising you with a stunning hidden courtyard or a glimpse of the sparkling sea. My best advice? Embrace becoming lost. Seriously. Put down the map for a while (though having one is useful for finally finding your way back!) and simply roam. This is where the magic occurs. You'll stumble across minor features you'd otherwise miss — an antique coat of arms above a doorway, a cat dozing on a sun-warmed step, the aroma of someone's lunch drifting from an open window. Wear comfortable shoes, as the stones have been polished by centuries of walking and can be a little slippery.

Key Areas of the Old Town

Even inside this little island, there are a few important reference points. The major square, **Trg Ivana Pavla II (Pope John Paul II Square)**, is the indisputable heart. Here you'll discover the majestic **St. Lawrence Cathedral**, the

Town Loggia, and the **Clock Tower**. It's the huge stage of Trogir. Running along to the southern tip of the island is the **Riva**, the popular beachfront promenade packed with cafés, restaurants, and bobbing boats. This is the place to go people-watching and soaking up the sun. The **Kamerlengo Fortress** anchors the southwestern point, a towering stone behemoth giving excellent vistas. Don't forget to explore the calmer northern and eastern areas of the island too; they often hold some of the most charming and serene locations.

Čiovo Island's Beaches, Bays, and Modern Trogir

Čiovo, pronounced CHEE-oh-voh, is located across the bridge from the Old Town. This considerably bigger island is home to the majority of Trogir's beaches, more contemporary residential areas, and a slightly different, more relaxed tourist mood. It's conveniently accessible and offers a nice contrast to the Old Town's historic intensity. Many people stay on Čiovo for its coastal lodgings and then head across to the Old Town to explore.

Arbanija and Slatine: Coastal Charms

As you go east from the bridge along Čiovo's northern shore, you will see communities such as **Arbanija** and **Slatine**.

These places are recognized for their numerous little pebble beaches, clear waters, and a more laid-back, family-oriented environment. There are several apartments for rent in this area, many of which have stunning views of the sea. Slatine, in particular, offers a charming little port and some beautiful coves to explore. It feels a little more "away from it all" yet still conveniently close.

Okrug Gornji & Donji: Lively Hubs

Okrug Gornji and **Okrug Donji** are located to the west and south of the bridge connecting to Čiovo, respectively. Okrug Gornji, often known as "Okrug," is the livelier hub, most noted for its long pebble beach, Copacabana (yes, truly!). This region is busy in the summer with beach bars, water sports, and a colorful vacation vibe. Okrug Donji is a bit quieter and offers more secluded bays if you're looking to escape the crowds. Both districts feature a good selection of hotels, restaurants, and shopping.

MAINLAND TROGIR: LOCAL LIFE AND PRACTICALITY

Don't overlook the mainland area of Trogir! This is where you'll find the major bus terminal, larger stores, the lively daily market (Pazar), and more residential neighborhoods where people live and work. While it may not have the same obvious historical appeal as the Old Town, it is an integral element of the Trogir experience. This is where you may see regular Croatian life unfold. If you're driving, you'll also find the majority of the bigger parking lots, as parking in or around the Old Town is highly scarce and can be expensive.

I often take a stroll through the market; it's an excellent place to buy fresh local produce and get a sense of the town's pulse.

SAFETY IN TROGIR: SAFE ZONES AND BEING STREET SMART

Now, let us talk safety. The good news is that Trogir is normally relatively safe, and Croatia as a whole has a low crime rate. I've always felt safe roaming around, even in the evenings. The residents are kind, and there is a strong sense of belonging. However, as with any popular tourist destination, being street smart pays off.

General Safety Tip

The standard common-sense guidelines apply: keep an eye on your possessions, especially in busy situations. Do not leave valuables unattended on the beach or visible in your vehicle. Be mindful of your surroundings, especially if you are out late. Stick to well-lit places at night, however even the smaller lanes in the Old Town are relatively secure. It's usually a good idea to carry travel insurance that includes theft protection just in case.

Areas Requiring Extra Awareness (e.g., busy pickpocketing spots)

The busiest places will, naturally, need you to be extra cautious. Think the **Riva promenade** at peak hours, the busy **main square** in the Old Town when tour groups are passing through, and the **market on the mainland**. These are great sites for opportunistic pickpockets. It's not a common problem by any means, but it's important to keep your wallet secure (maybe in a front pocket or a money belt) and be cautious of your luggage. Keep your bag where you can see it when you're seated at an outdoor café rather of slinging it over the back of your chair. To be honest, simply being smart and alert will most likely result in a trouble-free visit. Trogir is more about soaking in the scenery than worrying about crime.

Wrapping Up

So, there you have it—a short tour of Trogir's layout. Understanding these various zones will allow you to plan your days, select your lodging, and make the most of this incredible corner of Croatia. Next, we'll get into planning your actual adventure!

Chapter 3

PLANNING YOUR TROGIR ADVENTURE: BEFORE YOU GO.

Consider this chapter as a pre-flight checklist for Trogir. We'll go over the main topics, such as when to leave, what important documents you'll need, how much money to bring, and what on earth to pack in that luggage. Get them properly, and you're halfway to Trogir happiness.

WHEN TO VISIT TROGIR THROUGHOUT THE SEASONS

Ah, the everlasting question of any destination! The reality is that Trogir has its attractions all year round, although the "best" period depends on your preferences. I've visited in many seasons, and each provides its own distinctive taste.

Spring (April-May): Blooming Beauty & Mild Weather

Spring in Dalmatia, and Trogir in particular, is rather spectacular in my opinion. The countryside is alive with wildflowers, the air is crisp, and the temps are delightfully mild - perfect for exploring those ancient passageways without breaking a sweat. Because the tourist throngs haven't yet descended, you'll frequently feel as if you have more room to breathe and really enjoy the atmosphere. This is an excellent time to hike on Čiovo or visit national parks like Krka, when waterfalls are generally at their peak. If your schedule is right, you might be able to attend some great Easter events. Accommodation prices are often cheaper than in high summer also. The sea may still be too cold for some to swim in for lengthy periods of time, but it is certainly warming up!

Summer (June–August): Sun, Sea, and Festivals

There is little question that Trogir has reached its height. If you envision long, languid days on the beach, swimming in crystal-clear turquoise waters, and colorful nights packed with al fresco eating and crowded cafés, summer is the season for you. The weather is consistently hot and sunny, occasionally quite hot, and the Adriatic is delightfully pleasant. The Trogir Cultural Summer Festival is generally in full flow, and they offer music, folklore, and outdoor acts. The Riva promenade buzzes with vitality, while the adjacent islands and bays are perfect for boat expeditions. What's the downside? It's the busiest and most costly period. You'll need to reserve accommodations and popular tours ahead of time.

However, if you enjoy the bustling vacation atmosphere and can take the heat and crowds, summer in Trogir is an incredible delight.

Autumn (September-October): Pleasant Temperatures and Harvest Season

For many, like me, fall is the ideal time to visit Trogir. The searing heat of summer has subsided, leaving behind delightfully pleasant, sunny days and cooler, more comfortable evenings. Even in October, the sea is usually warm enough to swim. The summer throngs have reduced dramatically, allowing us a more unhurried exploration of the Old Town. It's also harvest season in Dalmatia, so you could see local festivals celebrating the abundance, and it's a great time for wine sampling. The light in October is also very lovely, giving a golden shine over the ancient stones. Accommodation prices also begin to fall. It's an ideal combination of pleasant weather, less people, and much to see and do.

Winter (November–March): Quiet Charm and Local Festivities

Winter in Trogir is a whole other experience. It is quiet. Very quiet. Many tourist-oriented restaurants and shops will close, particularly in January and February. However, if you're searching for an authentic, local experience and a calm vacation, it can be really unique. You'll have the Old Town almost to yourself, which is ideal for photography or just relaxing wandering. There may be some wonderful crisp, bright days, but be prepared for the **bura**, a powerful, cold wind that can blow down the coast. Around Christmas and New Year, there may be some festive lights and local festivals that offer a look into Croatian traditions. It's undoubtedly the most cost-effective time to visit. Simply pack warm clothing and ready for a much slower pace of life.

ESSENTIAL PRE-TRIP CHECKLIST: VISAS, INSURANCE, AND DOCUMENTS

Okay, let's talk about paperwork. Boring, I know, but totally necessary!

Passports and Visas: Croatia is a member of the EU and the Schengen Area. Many nationalities (including the United States, Canada, the United Kingdom, Australia, New Zealand, and other EU countries) do not require a visa for tourist stays of up to 90 days within 180 days. However, always check the official Croatian Ministry of Foreign and

European Affairs website well in advance to confirm the specific requirements for your nationality. Ensure that your passport is valid for at least six months beyond your intended stay. Years ago, I had a near-miss with passport validity, and believe me, that is not the kind of stress you need before a vacation!

Travel Insurance: Non-negotiable. I repeat, non-negotiable! Get complete travel insurance that includes medical emergencies (including repatriation), trip cancellation/interruption, lost baggage, and theft. Perhaps you will never need it, but if anything goes wrong, you'll be extremely thankful to have it.

Driving Documents: If you intend to rent a car (which can be great for day trips), make sure you have a valid driver's license. An International Driving Permit (IDP) is generally recommended and occasionally necessary, especially if your license isn't in English or doesn't utilize the Latin alphabet. Check with your rental car provider beforehand.

Booking Confirmations: Print down or save digital copies of your airline confirmations, hotel reservations, and any pre-booked tours or transfers. It's helpful to have them immediately available.

Emergency Information: Make a note of the contact information for your embassy in Croatia, your travel insurance emergency line, and maybe a local contact if you have one.

BUDGETING YOUR TRIP: FROM SHOESTRING TO SPLENDOR

Croatia, including Trogir, uses the euro (€). While it is not the most affordable location in Europe, it can nonetheless offer exceptional value, particularly when compared to several Western European destinations. Your travel preferences will have a significant impact on your budget.

Shoestring Traveler: You can absolutely do Trogir on a small budget. Think hostels (about €20-€40 a night), self-catering most of your meals by purchasing at the local Pazar market and supermarkets (fresh bread, cheese, fruits – great and inexpensive!), focusing on free activities like strolling the Old Town, swimming at public beaches, and enjoying the atmosphere. You could certainly manage on €50-€70 per day if you're cautious.

Mid-Range Traveler: This is probably where most tourists fall. Comfortable private rooms or apartments (Airbnb is popular) could price €70-€150+ per night depending on location and season. You can combine dining out at local konobas (a nice supper may cost €20-€40 per person) with self-catering. Consider any admission fees for sights (such as the Cathedral or Kamerlengo Fortress, which often cost a few Euros apiece) and a boat ride (€30-€60+). I'd budget roughly €100-€180 per person each day for a nice mid-range experience.

Luxury Splurge: If you're seeking to splurge, Trogir has possibilities! Boutique hotels in the Old Town and villas with pools on Čiovo can cost €200 to €500+ per night. Fine dining experiences, private boat tours, and skippered yacht charters will increase the cost. For a luxury trip, the sky is the limit, but budget for €250 or more per person per day.

Here are a few money-saving ideas from an old hand: Travel during the shoulder seasons (spring/autumn) to get better prices on lodging. Look for marenda or gablec (lunch specials) at local eateries, which are sometimes a great deal. Remember, strolling around and taking in the atmosphere is free!

What to Pack for Sun, Sea, and Sightseeing.

Smart layering and an embrace of the beach lifestyle are key when packing for Trogir.

Clothing: Light, breathable textiles are your greatest friend, especially during the summer (cotton, linen).

- Swimwear (plural: one to wear and one to dry!)
- Shorts, t-shirts, and tank tops.
- A few light long-sleeved shirts for sun protection and chilly evenings.
- One or two sundresses, or casual skirts.
- If you intend to attend finer meals, bring one or two somewhat more formal clothing.
- Even in the heat, wear a lightweight jacket or cardigan. Evenings along the sea can get a little windy, and it's handy for overly air-conditioned establishments or boat cruises. In spring/autumn, a warmer jacket or fleece is required.

Footwear: This is Crucial!

Comfortable Walking Shoes: Absolutely non-negotiable. The cobblestones of the Old Town are lovely, but they can be dangerous for your feet if you're not prepared. Consider sturdy trainers or comfy walking sandals.

Sandals/flip-flops: For beach and casual use.

Water Shoes: Because Croatian beaches are frequently pebbled, wearing water shoes can make entering the sea much more comfortable.

Sun Protection: The Dalmatian sun is really powerful!

- High SPF sunscreen (preferably reef-safe).
- Sunglasses.
- A broad brimmed hat.

Essentials and Technology:

- Passport, travel papers, and insurance information.
- Euros (cash for small transactions; cards are generally accepted).
- European plug adaptor (type C/F).
- Phone and charger, maybe a portable power bank.
- Camera to catch all of that splendor!

Toiletries and Medicines:

Your standard toiletries (travel-size to save space and weight).

Any prescribed drugs, including a copy of the prescription.

A small first-aid kit including basics such as plasters, pain medications, and antiseptic wipes.

Nice-to-Haves:

- Reusable water bottle (keep hydrated while reducing plastic waste).
- A small daypack to hold necessities while exploring.
- An excellent novel to read when sitting by the sea.

If you prefer exploring underwater, bring your snorkel gear; the Adriatic is stunningly clean.

What is my golden packing rule? Lay out everything you think you need, then return half of it! You'll thank me later when you're not dragging a heavy bag across those lovely but uneven cobblestones.

Wrapping Up

Phew! That's a lot to think about, but trust me when I say that putting these elements in order ahead of time will allow you to hit the ground running (or walking, Trogir-style) the moment you arrive. Now, are you ready to discuss what you plan to do when you arrive?

Chapter 4

Arriving and Moving Around: Transportation in Trogir

Getting to Trogir is typically easy, especially during the warmer months, and getting about after you've settled is also simple. Here's my opinion on the best ways to arrive and explore.

TRANSPORTATION TO TROGIR: BY AIR, SEA, BUS, AND CAR

Trogir is well-connected, so you have a few options depending on where you're coming from and your travel preferences.

Flights to Split Airport (SPU) and Transfers

This is by far the most popular route for foreign guests to come, and it's quite handy because **Split Airport (SPU)** is closer to Trogir than Split itself! We're only talking about 5-6 kilometers (3-4 miles) away. I've flown in here several times, and everything runs smoothly.

Once you land, going to Trogir is simple:

Taxi/Ride-Share: The quickest and most direct alternative. Taxis will be waiting outside the terminal. Expect to spend between €15 and €25 for the short journey, depending on traffic and time of day. Uber and Bolt also operate here and can sometimes be a bit cheaper.

Local Bus: The most cost-effective option. Bus route **No. 37** travels between Split Airport, Trogir, and Split city. The stop is directly on the main road outside the airport terminal. It's incredibly inexpensive (only a handful of Euros), but it makes more stops, so it'll take a bit longer (maybe 15-20 minutes to Trogir). The pre-booked transfer will drop you off at Trogir's major bus terminal on the mainland, just a short walk from the Old Town. For maximum peace of mind, especially if you're traveling late or with plenty of bags, you can pre-book a private shuttle. Many hotels and apartment owners offer this service, or you can use numerous internet sites.

Ferry and Catamaran

If you're already traveling between islands along the Dalmatian coast or coming from Split, arriving by sea is a stunningly picturesque choice, but direct ferry services to

Trogir proper are less regular than to Split. Most coastal ferries and catamarans (including those from Jadrolinija and Kapetan Luka) will dock in Split. From Split's ferry port, you can easily take the aforementioned bus No. 37 or a taxi to Trogir (about a 30--40-minute ride).

The **Bura Line** provides a local passenger boat service connecting Split Riva, Slatine (on Čiovo), and Trogir. This is a beautiful, slow method to get between these locations, and it offer excellent vistas. It's more of a scenic route than a quick commute, but I highly recommend it if you have the time.

Intercity Buses and Driving to Trogir

Croatia has an excellent and reasonably priced intercity bus network. Arriving by bus from other Croatian cities such as Zagreb, Zadar, or Dubrovnik, or even adjacent countries, is an excellent choice. Buses will take you to Trogir's main bus terminal on the mainland, which is just a stone's throw from the Old Town Bridge.

Driving to Trogir Allows you greatest freedom, especially when exploring the surrounding area. Croatia boasts wonderful contemporary freeways (with tolls). The main A1 motorway runs along the coastline. From the Prgomet exit, the trip to Trogir is easy. Just be aware that parking in Trogir can be difficult, which we will discuss later!

NAVIGATING TROGIR AND ČIOVO:

Once in Trogir, traveling about is mainly enjoyable, especially since the most picturesque portion is car-free!

Walking: The Best Way to Explore the Old Town

Let me be clear: walking is *the* way to enjoy Trogir's Old Town. Its small, meandering lanes, secret courtyards, and beautiful squares were ideal for ambling. The whole Old Town is pedestrian-only, and it's small enough that you can traverse much of it on foot without feeling fatigued (though those cobblestones will give your calf muscles a mild workout!). This is where you'll make your finest discoveries, so pack those comfy shoes I keep suggesting!

Local Buses and Water Taxis

To explore farther away, especially on Čiovo island or to get to adjacent beaches, local buses are an alternative. Buses can be taken from Trogir's main bus terminal to many settlements on Čiovo, including Okrug Gornji and Slatine.

They're inexpensive and typically dependable, however timetables can be more 'flexible' in the off-season.

Water taxis are a terrific and enjoyable way to travel about, especially between Trogir Riva and other spots on Čiovo, such as Okrug Gornji's Copacabana beach or Slatine. In the summer, they offer regular service, offer picturesque vistas, and alleviate traffic congestion on iovo. Look for little boats zipping back and forth from the Riva.

Renting Scooters, Bicycles, and Cars

Scooters are an extremely popular alternative, especially for getting around Čiovo. They make parking easier and are great for getting between beaches and exploring the island's nooks and crannies. You may discover rental options in Trogir and Čiovo. Simply make sure you're comfortable riding one, and always wear a helmet.

Bicycles: Ideal for shorter journeys and exploring flat regions. Čiovo offers scenic coastal paths, but the terrain can be hilly in spots.

Cars: Renting a car is great for day trips outside of Trogir, such as to Krka National Park or ibenik. However, driving around Trogir and Čiovo can be challenging due to traffic and parking restrictions. If you do rent one, consider picking it up only on the days you intend to travel further.

Parking in and around Trogir is an issue in European medieval cities.

Old Town: Forget it. It is only open to pedestrians.

Mainland Trogir: There are numerous huge pay-and-display parking lots on the mainland, immediately before the bridge to the Old Town. These are your best options if you're driving in for the day. Prices vary, and they can fill up quickly in the summer. Parking is typically less expensive the further you park from the bridge.

Čiovo Island: Most accommodations on Čiovo have parking. If not, street parking can be difficult and frequently restricted. There are some public lots near popular beaches like Okrug Gornji, but again, they get busy.

Insider Tip: If you can avoid having a car for the days, you're entirely focused on Trogir and immediate Čiovo, do it. If you need one for day visits, attempt to park it on the mainland and stroll into the Old Town. Patience is a virtue when it comes to Trogir parking during peak season!

Wrapping Up

So, there you have it! Getting to and around Trogir is all part of the trip. A little forethought, some comfy shoes, and possibly a desire to get on a local boat or bus, and you'll be traveling this gorgeous area of Croatia like a genuine tourist.

Chapter 5

TROGIR'S TOP TEN ICONIC LANDMARKS AND MONUMENTS.

Prepare to travel back in time as we discover the best of Trogir's architectural and historical treasures. These aren't just old structures; they're storytellers, each with their own distinct tale to tell.

Saint Lawrence Cathedral with Radovan's Portal (Katedrala Sv. Lovre)

Location: Trg Ivana Pavla II (Pope John Paul II Square) is the principal square in the heart of Trogir's Old Town. You simply cannot miss it.

Cost of Entry: The Cathedral often charges a small entrance fee of roughly 5-7 Euros. This charge usually includes entry to the Baptistery and the Treasury. Climbing the Bell Tower normally costs an additional small charge (about 2-3 Euros). Prices can change somewhat.

Details: This is unquestionably Trogir's most stunning building. Construction began around 1213 and lasted for centuries, resulting in a stunning combination of Romanesque and Gothic styles. The main entrance, Radovan's Portal, was carved by Master Radovan in 1240 and is the true showpiece. It's a true masterwork of medieval sculpture, representing scenes from the Bible, allegorical figures, and everyday life in stunning detail. I could stand and look at it for an hour. Inside, the lofty nave, finely carved choir stalls, and the stunning Chapel of St. John of Trogir (Ivan Ursini) are breathtaking. If you have the opportunity, climb the Bell Tower; the panoramic views of the red-tiled rooftops of the Old Town and the shimmering Adriatic are well worth the effort.

Special Entry Requirements:

Dress Code: Because this is an active place of worship, modest attire is needed. The shoulders and knees should be covered. Shawls or wraps are frequently available at the entrance.

Photography: Often permitted indoors without flash, but please be mindful of services or worshipers.

Pets: Not permitted within the Cathedral.

Alcohol/Smoking: Strictly banned.

Accessibility: The main floor is generally accessible, but the Bell Tower and some other areas require numerous stairs.

KAMERLENGO FORTRESS, GUARDIAN OF THE COAST (KAŠTEL KAMERLENGO)

Location: On the southwestern corner of Trogir's Old Town island, facing the sea channel and Riva promenade.

Address: Obala Bana Berislavića, 21220, Trogir.

Entry Fee: Usually approximately 4-5 euros.

Details: The Venetians erected this strong fortification in the mid-15th century, and it feels right out of a storybook. Its strong stone walls and majestic towers were built to safeguard the sea channel and Trogir harbor. You can stroll around its walls, look through the arrow holes, and picture the sentries who once stood guard. The views from the summit are breathtaking, offering a fresh viewpoint on the Old Town, Čiovo Island, and the bustling waterfront. In the summer, the fortress's courtyard frequently hosts open-air concerts, film screenings, and theatrical events, creating a wonderful atmosphere.

Special Entry Requirements:

Photography: Allowed.

Pets: Not permitted within the paid sections.

Alcohol/Smoking: Prohibited, except in designated areas during events.

Accessibility: The ramparts are reached via uneven surfaces and numerous stairs; those with mobility issues may find it difficult to access.

THE TOWN LOGGIA AND CLOCK TOWER (GRADSKA LOŽA, TORANJ SA SATOM)

Location: Dominating one side of Trg Ivana Pavla II, near the Cathedral.

Address: Trg Ivana Pavla II, 21220 Trogir.

Cost of Entry: The Loggia is an open-air construction; thus, it is free to watch and sit in. The Clock Tower is not usually open for climbing.

Details: The Loggia, which dates back to the 14th or 15th century, was once the public courthouse and a venue for important public announcements and meetings. Notice the gorgeous Renaissance relief by Ivan Meštrović (a modern addition portraying Petar Berislavić, a Croatian Ban and bishop), as well as the earlier reliefs by Nikola Firentinac. It's a great place to sit for a moment and take in the atmosphere of the square, imagining the centuries of public life that have unfolded here. The adjacent Clock Tower, which was once part of the Church of St. Sebastian, is a prominent landmark of the area, with its vivid blue clock face.

Special Entry Requirements: As an open public place, it is normally accessible at all times. Show respect for its historical significance.

Pets: Allowed in the open Loggia area if they are well-behaved and on a leash.

Alcohol/Smoking: Not allowed in the immediate historical area, though cafes are nearby.

Cipiko Palaces (Palača Ćipiko).

Location: Trg Ivana Pavla II is located just across from St. Lawrence Cathedral's main entrance.

Address: Trg Ivana Pavla II, 21220 Trogir.

Cost of Entry: These are predominantly private dwellings or companies presently; therefore, you generally appreciate them from the exterior for free. Occasionally, portions could be available for special exhibitions or events, although this isn't usual.

Details: During the Venetian era, one of Trogir's most prominent noble families owned two Cipiko Palaces, one large and one small. The Large Cipiko Palace, which faces the Cathedral, is an outstanding example of Venetian Gothic architecture, with its ornate triple-arched windows (a trifora) and lovely balconies. Imagine the magnificent parties and celebrations that formerly took place within these walls! Look for Alviz Ćipiko's wooden sculpture of a cockerel recovered from a Turkish ship during a naval combat. You can truly sense the riches and power of the family that shaped Trogir here.

Special Entry Requirements: Because these are mostly private, please respect the residents' privacy. Admire from the square.

TOWN GATES: KOPNENA VRATA (LAND GATE) AND MORSKA VRATA (SEA GATE).

Location: The Land Gate located on the northern side of the Old Town, linking to the mainland bridge. The Sea Gate is located on the southern side and opens onto the Riva.

Address: Land Gate: Ulica hrvatskih mučenika, 21220 Trogir. Sea Gate: Obala bana Berislavića, 21220 Trogir.

Cost of Entry: Free. These are public thoroughfares.

Details: These were formerly the primary entrances into the walled Old Town. The Land Gate (Kopnena Vrata), also known as the North Gate, is spectacular with its Renaissance arch and the statue of St. John of Trogir (Ivan Ursini), the town's patron saint, watching over it. Passing through it definitely seems like stepping back in time. The Sea Gate (Morska Vrata), or South Gate, dates back to the 16th century and connects straight to the lively Riva. Imagine centuries of merchants and sailors passing through these gates.

Special Entry Requirements:

None, as these are public access points. Just be mindful of foot traffic.

Benedictine Monastery of St. Nicholas and Kairos Collection

Location: Secluded on the southern side of the Old Town, close to the Kamerlengo Fortress. Look for signs.

Address: Gradskavrata 4, 21220 Trogir.

Entry Fee: About 3-4 Euros to visit the Kairos Collection.

Details: The Kairos relief, one of Trogir's most valuable treasures, is housed in this active Benedictine nunnery, which dates back to the 11th century. This beautiful Greek marble slab from the third or fourth century BC depicts Kairos, the deity of the opportune time. It is extremely delicate and well-preserved, making it a must-see for anybody interested in ancient art. The monastery is a calm haven, and the sisters occasionally offer handcrafted crafts or liqueurs.

Special Entry Requirements:

Dress Code: Please dress modestly.

Photography: There may be restrictions in the Kairos Collection area; always ask.

Pets: Not permitted.

Alcohol/Smoking: Prohibited.

Remember that this is a functioning monastery, so keep a respectful silence.

Saint Dominic's Church and Monastery (Crkva i Samostan Sv. Dominika)

Location: At the western end of the Riva promenade, near Kamerlengo.

Address: Obala Bana Berislavića, 21220, Trogir.

Cost of Entry: Usually free to visit the church, however gifts are accepted. There can be a small cost if there's a special display in the monastery area.

Details: Founded in the 13th century, this complex contains a basic yet attractive Gothic church. In the monastery area, you can see intriguing tombs, altarpieces, and a lovely courtyard. It's a lovely area situated on the bustling Riva, offering a moment of silence and thought. Its modest beauty contrasts nicely with the Cathedral's grandeur.

Special Entry Requirements:

Dress code: For church, wear something modest.

Pets: Not permitted inside.

Alcohol/smoking: prohibited.

TROGIR TOWN MUSEUM (MUSEJ GRADA TROGIRA)

Housed in the stunning Garagnin-Fanfogna Palace, just off the main square.

Address: Gradska vrata 4, 21220 Trogir (this address is frequently cited as being close to the Benedictine Monastery, but check locally as it is part of a palace complex). It's very close to the North Gate.

Entry Fee: Around 3-5 euros.

Details: If you want a deeper dive into Trogir's rich history, here is the spot. The museum shows archeological artifacts, historical documents, period furniture, portraits, and objects relating to the town's aristocratic families and maritime heritage. The edifice itself, a Romanesque-Baroque palace, is worth seeing. It gives an excellent background for everything else you'll see in the Old Town.

Special Entry Requirements:

Photography: Usually permitted, but check with specific exhibits.

Pets: Not permitted.

Alcohol/smoking: Prohibited.

Bags: You might be asked to leave larger bags at the entrance.

THE RIVA PROMENADE: HEART OF TROGIR

Location: The large, palm-lined waterfront promenade on the southern edge of the Old Town island.

Address: Obala Bana Berislavića, 21220, Trogir.

Fee: There is no entry fee. It is a public place.

Details: This isn't a single monument, rather it's an unforgettable Trogir experience. The Riva is Trogir's living room. It's where people and visitors go to stroll (the renowned korzo), drink coffee at one of the many cafés, eat ice cream, or simply watch the yachts and fishing boats bobbing in the port. With Kamerlengo Fortress at one end and views across to Čiovo Island, it's tremendous picturesque, especially at sunset. It's humming with life from dawn till late at night.

Special Entry Requirements:

None. Enjoy responsibly! Be mindful of restaurant seating.

Pets: Welcome on leashes.

Alcohol/smoking: permitted in designated outdoor cafe/bar areas.

MARMONT'S GLORIETTE (GLORIJET MARMONT).

Location: On the westernmost tip of the Old Town island, between the Kamerlengo Fortress and St. Mark's Tower.

Address: Setaliste Stjepana Radica, 21220 Trogir.

Entry Fee: There is no entry fee. It's an open-air monument.

Details: This magnificent Neoclassical pavilion, with its six stone columns, was erected in the early 19th century during the brief French administration under Napoleon's Marshal Marmont. It was intended as a monument to glorify French rule but also served as a rather pleasant spot for officers to relax. It's a lovely, slightly more tranquil place to sit and enjoy the sea views, often with fewer people than the main Riva. It makes a nice contrast with the older Venetian architecture.

Special Entry Requirements:

None. It is a public place.

Wrapping Up

There you have it - my top 10 recommendations to actually go to the heart of Trogir's ancient magnificence. Each one is a jewel, and collectively they offer a memorable image of this magnificent town. Enjoy your excursions!

Chapter 6

BEYOND THE POSTCARDS: OFF-THE-BEATEN-PATH TROGIR & HIDDEN GEMS

You have strolled down the busy Riva and seen the gorgeous cathedral. Let's take a closer look and find the Trogir that speaks in whispers instead of shouts. These are my personal favorites; you can usually find some tranquility there as well as a stronger sense of the town's genuine character.

THE OLD TOWN'S HIDDEN COURTYARDS AND ALLEYWAYS

For me, this is where the true charm of exploring Trogir is found. While the major streets are lovely, true magic is discovered when you swerve down a seemingly unimportant alleyway. There are small, sunlit courtyards where potted plants tumble over old stone, laundry flutters between houses like vibrant flags, and the only sound may be a cat stretching or a distant conversation. For this type of aimless exploring, the Old Town's eastern and northern sections are especially suitable. Don't be scared to get "lost"; you can't go too far on a small island, and every unexpected turn frequently results in a fascinating discovery. The ages seem to fade away in these peaceful nooks.

LITTLE-KNOWN CHAPELS AND CHURCHES (LIKE ST. PETER AND ST. BARBARA)

Trogir is home to numerous smaller, frequently disregarded churches and chapels that have a distinct beauty of their own, even while St. Lawrence Cathedral rightfully takes center stage. Tucked away next to the Land Gate is Trogir's oldest preserved church, the little Church of St. Barbara (Sveti Barbara), which dates back to the ninth century.

It is very poignant in its pre-Romanesque simplicity. The Church of St. Peter (Sveti Petar), which was once a Benedictine nunnery, is another treasure. It has a remarkable wooden roof and a lovely Baroque interior. These are private areas that offer a sense of peace and an alternative viewpoint on Trogir's spiritual legacy. You'll often have them to yourself.

Finding Artisan Workshops in the Area

You can stumble across small workshops where local craftspeople are preserving traditional crafts tucked away in those winding lanes. I've discovered small jewelry stores with meticulously crafted filigree, artists' studios featuring one-of-a-kind ceramics or paintings influenced by the local landscape, and even stores that sell traditional Dalmatian linens or handcrafted leather products. These aren't your average souvenir shops; they offer a chance to discover something genuinely original and to engage with Trogir's creative energy. Keep an eye out and don't be afraid to stop by; the craftspeople tend to be delighted to discuss their creations. It's a fantastic way to help out local artists.

Undiscovered Beaches and Coves on Čiovo Island

Even if Okrug Gornji's "Copacabana" is vibrant and enjoyable, Čiovo has a lot to offer if, like me, you occasionally yearn for a more sedate area with pebbles and crystal-clear water. Explore the island's shoreline by renting a scooter or perhaps a bicycle, or simply be ready for a short walk. Explore the southern part of the island or head east toward

Slatine and beyond. There are several of smaller coves where you can get away from the people, some of which are reachable by narrow dirt tracks. For those looking for something a little more rustic, Kava Beach, which is close to Slatine, is well-liked. The peace and stunning environment make the effort worthwhile, but bring some water and food as amenities may be limited.

A COASTAL WETLAND PARADISE: PANTAN NATURE RESERVE

This very little natural reserve is located near the point where the Pantan River joins the sea, a short distance east of Trogir. This rocky area is home to a rare coastal wetland that serves as a refuge for birds, particularly during migration seasons. The attractiveness is enhanced by the presence of a historic fortified Renaissance mill. A calm stroll, some birdwatching, or simply a respite from the Old Town's historic stone can be found here. From Trogir, it's conveniently accessible by quick cab ride, or even a delightful longer stroll or bike ride. It serves as a reminder of this historic town's surrounding natural splendor.

Exploring the quieter parts of Mainland Trogir

The Old Town island is, understandably, the main attraction for most tourists. Beyond the immediate area of the market and bus terminal, however, Trogir's mainland portion has its own distinct local character. You may observe Croatian daily life as it unfolds on the residential streets, with children playing, neighbors conversing over garden fences, and the aroma of home cooking filling the air.

Here, paying attention to the local rhythm is more important than seeing certain "sights." It provides a more comprehensive view of Trogir as a vibrant community rather than only a travel destination. Additionally, there may be some great, modest local bakeries or cafes that serve locals rather than visitors.

Chapter 7

EXCITING ADVENTURES & MEMORABLE MOMENTS

Alright, so you've learned about the past and discovered some undiscovered treasures. Are you prepared for a little cultural immersion and action now? Trogir is a great starting point for a variety of activities, both on and off the water, so it's not only about admiring ancient stones!

WATER SPORTS: JET SKIING, PADDLEBOARDING, KAYAKING, AND SAILING

With the Adriatic shining all around, it would be a crime to stay off the water! Trogir and Čiovo are popular destinations for a variety of water sports.

Sailing: Trogir is a well-liked starting location for charters, and the Dalmatian coast is a sailor's dream. You can participate in a skippered day trip even if you're not an experienced sailor.

Kayaking & Paddleboarding (SUP): One of my favorite slower-paced methods to explore the coastline is via kayaking and paddleboarding (SUP). You can paddle into secret coves, explore sea caves, or simply take in the tranquility by renting kayaks or SUPs from numerous beaches on iovo. There are also guided tours offered.

Jet Skiing: Larger beaches like Okrug Gornji offer jet ski rentals for those seeking a little more excitement. It's a lot of fun, but pay attention to swimmers and authorized places.

SNORKELING AND DIVING: DISCOVERING THE ADRIATIC SEA'S UNDERWATER WORLD

Numerous beaches in the Trogir area offer great snorkeling due to the waters' exceptional clarity. You'll be amazed at the variety of marine creatures you may see if you simply put on a mask and fins. PADI training and guided dives to neighboring reefs, wrecks, and under water caverns are offered by various dive shops in Trogir and on iovo for a more immersive experience. Even while the Adriatic lacks the tropics' technicolor coral, its underwater scenery and purity are stunning.

Boat Trips: Drvenik Islands, Šolta, and Blue Lagoon

You must do this! The Trogir Riva offers a great day out, with many boat tours departing from it. On the island of Drvenik Veli, the Blue Lagoon (Krknjaši Bay) is a popular destination because of its crystal-clear turquoise water, which is ideal for swimming and snorkeling. Many tours also include stops on the nearby Drvenik islands or the island of olta for lunch or exploring its quaint settlements.

There are smaller, more personal boat cruises in addition to larger group tours. For me, a trip to Trogir would not be complete without spending a day on the water exploring these neighboring islands.

Hiking and Cycling Trails on Čiovo and the mainland

There are some great places to stretch your legs if you want to go away from the sea. Numerous designated paths in Čiovo wind through pine forests and olive orchards, frequently offering breathtaking sweeping views of Trogir and the mainland. The surroundings of Slatine and the pilgrimage chapel of Gospa od Prizidnice (Our Lady of Prizidnica), which is set on a cliff, offer some excellent treks.

Exploring the hinterland of Dalmatia on the mainland can also show you another side of the region. Request trail maps from the local tourism office.

Cultural Immersion: Wine Tasting, Olive Oil Experiences, and Cooking Classes

You must taste a place in order to fully connect with it! And there's no better way than to get your hands dirty.

Cooking Classes: Discover how to make classic Dalmatian meals like fresh pasta with seafood or peka, which is meat or seafood slow-cooked under a metal dome. A market excursion is frequently included in the programs offered by various locations. It's a tasty and enjoyable experience.

Wine Tasting: The history of winemaking in Dalmatia is extensive. To try local varietals like Pošip (a crisp white) or Plavac Mali (a powerful red), look for nearby wineries or wine bars.

Experiences with Olive Oil: Croatian olive oil is of the highest caliber. You can sample various oils and learn about the production process by attending tastings and grove tours offered by some local producers. It's a true culinary delight.

Local Fishermen's Fishing Trips

Arrange a fishing excursion with a local fisherman for a completely genuine and remarkable experience. Some offer tours where you may spend a few hours, learn about traditional fishing methods, and hopefully catch your dinner! It's a great way to interact with Trogir's marine tradition and view the coast from a new angle. Since these aren't usually officially promoted, you might need to ask about at the harbor or through your lodging, but the experience is well worth the trouble.

Chapter 8

A CULINARY JOURNEY: TROGIR'S GASTRONOMICAL DELIGHTS

Prep your taste buds because Trogir provides a delightful tour through Adriatic flavors. It's all about fresh, seasonal ingredients, simple yet expert preparation, and the lovely Mediterranean mentality of sharing good food with good people.

THE FLAVORS OF DALMATIA: A GUIDE TO LOCAL CUISINE

Dalmatian cuisine represents the center of Mediterranean cuisine. picture sun-ripened vegetables, incredible olive oil (literally liquid gold here), fresh herbs like rosemary and sage, garlic (plenty of it, thankfully!), and, of course, an abundance of sea treasures. It is generally healthy, extremely flavorful, and frequently includes grilling (na gradele), stewing, or baking. You'll see influences from Italy (particularly Venice), but with a unique Croatian flavor.

Simplicity is crucial, and the quality of the ingredients shows through.

Must-Try Trogir Specialties. Peka, Pašticada and Fresh Seafood

If you want a genuine flavor of Trogir, look out for these:

Peka: This is iconic! Meat (often lamb or veal), shellfish, and vegetables are slowly cooked under a metal dome (the "peka") submerged in hot embers. The finished result is exceptionally delicate and delicious. You generally have to order it in advance, so ask your konoba.

Pašticada: is a renowned Dalmatian festive meal. Beef is marinated in vinegar and spices for hours or even days before slow-cooking with prunes, carrots, and prošek (sweet dessert wine) until it's tender. Typically served with handmade gnocchi. It's rich, complex, and very delicious.

Fresh Seafood: When you're this close to the sea, you have to indulge. Grilled fish (riba na gradele), simply seasoned with olive oil, garlic, and parsley, is a must. Another traditional dish is black risotto (crni rižot), which is dyed and flavored with cuttlefish ink. Simply ask your waiter what is freshest that day!

KONOBAS (TRADITIONAL TAVERNS): AUTHENTIC LOCAL CUISINE

For the most outstanding Trogir dining experience, visit a konoba. These are traditional Dalmatian taverns, most times family-owned, with tone walls, rustic charm, and a focus on lovely, home-style cooking. This is where you can get the best peka, homemade pasta, and grilled meats and fish made with love. Don't expect flashy decorations, just fantastic, honest food and a friendly welcome. When I arrive, I always head straight to a good konoba.

FINE DINING AND MODERN CROATIAN CUISINE.

While traditional food reigns supreme, Trogir is also home to a growing number of restaurants that serve a more refined, modern version of Croatian cuisine. These establishments often offer creative presentations and innovative flavor combinations wine lists. If you're looking for a special occasion meal or simply want to sample the contemporary culinary scene, there are some excellent options, particularly along the Riva or tucked away in elegant old town courtyards.

Casual Eats: Pizzerias, Cafes, and Street Food Gems

maybe you just want something quick, delicious and easy. Trogir delivers! You'll find plenty of pizzerias serving up tasty pies (Italian influence again!). Cafes are perfect for a sandwich, a light lunch, or a salad.

For street food, look for ćevapi (grilled minced meat sausages served in flatbread with onions and ajvar - a red pepper relish) or burek (a flaky pastry filled with meat or cheese, ideal for a cheap and cheerful snack from a local bakery or pekara).

Sweet Treats: Ice Cream, Fritule, and Local Desserts

Visiting the Adriatic without indulging in ice cream (sladoled) is a big miss out! Trogir has numerous gelaterias that offers a rainbow of flavors. During festive period, especially Christmas, look for fritule – little Croatian doughnuts, sometimes flavored with citrus zest and raisins, with powdered sugar dusted on it. They're amazingly addictive! Various restaurants also offer traditional desserts like rožata (a Dalmatian crème caramel) or simple cakes made with local fruits and nuts.

WINE BARS AND RAKIJA TASTING

Croatia has a fantastic, and most times underrated, wine scene. Trogir has various charming wine bars where you can sample local Dalmatian wines, from crisp whites like Pošip and Maraština to robust reds like Plavac Mali. It's an excellent way to spend an evening. try rakija for something a bit stronger. This is a local fruit brandy, and it comes in countless varieties – lozovača (grape), travarica (herb-infused), šljivovica (plum), orahovica (walnut). It's offered as a welcome drink or a digestif. It packs a punch, yet part of the local experience, so drink with caution! Živjeli! (Cheers!)

Wrapping Up

There you have it, ready for a treat, because Dalmatian food is something special, and Trogir is a fantastic place to dive in fork-first! For me, exploring the local cuisine is much important as seeing the sights – it's how you taste the soul of a place.

Chapter 9

ACCOMMODATION IN TROGIR

Let's explore where you might like to unload your luggage in and around this gorgeous town.

LUXURY STAYS: HOTELS AND HERITAGE PROPERTIES

For those wishing to indulge, Trogir offers some very remarkable high-end alternatives, typically marrying ancient beauty with modern luxury.

✓ **Brown Beach House & Spa (Old Town/Čiovo Bridge nearby)**

Vibe: Chic, modern decor with a vintage flair, magnificent pool area, and excellent spa. Ideal for couples and anyone seeking sophisticated relaxation.

Specifics:

Lovers: Luxurious rooms, spa services, and a romantic atmosphere.

Families: Some bigger rooms available, although mostly adult-focused.

Solo Travelers: Safe, elegant, with lots of facilities to enjoy.

Pet-friendly (please clarify policy and costs).

Price Range (estimated. per night): €200 - €500+

Address: Put Vlaka 6, 21220, Trogir (Technically on Čiovo, but immediately beside the bridge to the Old Town)

✓ Hotel Pašike (Old Town)

Vibe: Heritage hotel in a wonderfully renovated 19th-century structure with antiques and traditional charm. provides a genuine, historic luxury experience.

Specifics:

Lovers: Romantic and historic surroundings, as well as the distinctive accommodations.

Families: Some family rooms are available.

Solo Travelers: Charming and well positioned for exploration.

Pets: Confirm personally; policies may differ.

Price Range (estimated. per night): €150 to €350+

Address: Sinjska ul. 6, 21220 Trogir.

✓ Hotel Trogir Palace (Mainland, waterfront near the Old Town Bridge).

Vibe: A modern hotel with stunning views of the Old Town from across the sea. Provides pleasant accommodations, a good restaurant, and convenient access.

Specifics:

Lovers: Rooms with Old Town views are particularly charming.

Families: Family rooms and suites are offered.

Solo Travelers: It's comfortable and convenient.

Pet-friendly (please clarify policy and costs).

Price range (estimated. each night): €130 to €300+

Address: Put Cumbrijana 14, 21220 Trogir.

Boutique Hotels and Charming Guesthouses in the Old Town.

These provide a more personal and usually character-driven experience, right in the center of the action.

XII Century Heritage Hotel (Old Town).

Vibe: Small, wonderfully rebuilt hotel within a 12th-century structure, merging antique stone with modern conveniences. Very atmospheric.

Specifics:

Lovers: Extremely romantic, historical, and personal.

Solo Travelers: Safe, central, and full of personality.

Families: Due to the ancient building, there are few family room alternatives; couples or solitary travelers are better suited.

Pets: Unlikely due to historic nature; please confirm directly.

Price range (approx. per night): €120 to €280+

Address: Ulica Vinka Celija 2, 21220 Trogir.

✓ **Hotel Bifora (Old Town)**

Vibe: A charming family-run guesthouse/small hotel in a historic building noted for its courteous service and convenient location.

Specifics:

Lovers: Cozy and centrally situated for romantic strolls.

Solo Travelers: Friendly atmosphere, ideal base for exploration.

Families: Some bigger rooms may be available.

Pets: Please confirm immediately.

Price Range (estimated. each night): €90 to €200+

Address: Ribarska ul. 9, 21220 Trogir.

✓ **Heritage Hotel Tragos (Old Town)**

Vibe: Located in a 13th-century palace, with nicely designated apartments and a well-known restaurant. Combines heritage with comfort.

Specifics:

Lovers: historic charm and great dining on-site.

Solo Travelers: Safe, central, and culturally diverse.

Families: may have options, but they are best suited for couples.

Pets: Confirm personally; policies may differ.

Price Range (estimated. per night): €110 - €250+

Address: Budislavićeva ul. 1, 21220, Trogir

Mid-Range Comfort: Apartments and Private Rooms

This is usually the sweet spot for many tourists, giving decent pricing, additional space, and often cooking amenities. Platforms like Booking.com and Airbnb are your buddies here.

✓ **Apartments and rooms Trogir Stars (Old Town and nearby)**

Vibe: A collection of well-maintained flats and rooms in diverse places, many of them are modernly equipped and have decent amenities.

Specifics:

Families: Many flats provide numerous bedrooms and kitchens.

Lovers: Studios and one-bedroom flats provide seclusion.

Solo Travelers: may enjoy safe and convenient studio accommodations.

Pets: Some homes may allow pets; please verify individual listings.

Price range (estimated. each night): €70 to €180+

Addresses: Several places in and around the Old Town (see individual listing).

✓ **Villa Luna Trogir in Čiovo, near Okrug Gornji.**

Vibe: Modern apartment complex with a pool, popular with families and people looking for a beachfront location.

Specifics:

Families: Pool, self-catering, proximity to beaches.

Lovers: those who like apartments with balconies and sea views.

Solo Travelers: It may be a little family-oriented, but studio choices might work.

Pets: Check directly with the apartment owners.

Price Range (estimated. each night): €80 - €200+

Address: Put Diruna 63, 21223, Okrug Gornji, Čiovo

✓ **Guest House Mirkec (Mainland Trogir, short walk to Old Town)**

Vibe: A welcoming, family-run guesthouse with clean and comfortable rooms and flats at moderate rates.

Specifics:

Solo Travelers: Good value, friendly atmosphere.

Lovers: Private rooms with convenient access to Old Town.

Families: Some apartments are available.

Pets: Please confirm immediately.

Price range (estimated. each night): €60 to €150+

Address: Ulica Kardinala Alojzija Stepinca 10, 21220 Trogir.

BUDGET-FRIENDLY OPTIONS

Hostels and Affordable Rentals Exploring Trogir on a limited budget does not mean compromising comfort.

✓ **Hostel Trogir (Old Town)**

Vibe: A friendly and communal hostel located in the middle of the Old Town, with dorm beds and some private rooms. Perfect for meeting other tourists.

Specifics:

Solo Travelers: Ideal for socializing and cheap travel.

Pets: In general, dorm rooms are not suited for pets.

Families/Lovers: Private rooms may be available.

Price range (approx. per night): €20 to €50 (dorm bed); €50 to €80 (private room)

Address: Matije Gupca 10, 21220 Trogir.

✓ **City Hostel Trogir (Mainland, Near Bus Station)**

Vibe: A modern, clean hostel with excellent amenities, strategically located near the bus station and a short walk from the Old Town.

Specifics:

Solo Travelers: An excellent affordable choice for transit.

Pets: are seldom in shared dormitories.

Families and lovers: Private rooms may be available.

Price range (approx. per night): €20 to €45 (dorm bed).

Address: Ulica Kardinala Alojzija Stepinca 17, 21220 Trogir.

✓ **Private rooms ("Sobe") on Čiovo, including Okrug, Arbanija, and Slatine.**

Vibe: Renting a separate room in a local's house might be quite inexpensive. Look for "Sobe" indicators or consult online resources. Often modest yet clean, and provides a local feel.

Specifics:

Solo Travelers: Benefit from lower costs and more opportunities for local contact.

Lovers: Affordable private space.

Families: You may locate accommodations that may accommodate small families.

Pets are entirely up to the individual homeowner; always inquire.

Price range (estimated. each night): €30–€70+

Address: Various places in Čiovo.

UNIQUE ACCOMMODATIONS:

For something a bit different...

✓ **Villa rentals in Čiovo (e.g. Okrug Gornji, Mastrinka).**

Vibe: Renting a private villa, sometimes with a pool, is ideal for larger parties or families seeking space and seclusion.

Specifics:

Families/Groups: Perfect for self-catering and private pool use.

Lovers: A beautiful and exclusive hideaway (may be expensive for only two).

Pets: Many villas welcome pets; check individual listings.

Price Range (estimated. each night): €150 - €1000+ (depending on size and luxury)

Address: Several places on Čiovo.

✓ **Agroturizam inland from Trogir (for example, towards the hinterland of Seget Donji).**

Staying on a functioning farm or country estate provides an opportunity to experience rural Dalmatian life. Often includes home-cooked meals made using local vegetables. A tranquil getaway.

Specifics:

Lover/Family/Solo: Ideal for a calm, real encounter.

Pets: Because of the rural surroundings, pet-friendly accommodations are common; please confirm.

Price range (estimated. each night): €70 to €150+

Addresses: A variety of places in the hinterland (car required).

- ✓ Boat Stays and Yacht Charters (ACI Marina Trogir and Nearby Marinas)

Vibe: For a real nautical experience, stay aboard a marina boat or lease one (with or without a skipper).

Specifics:

Lovers: Extremely romantic and distinctive.

Families/Solo: Can be an experience, but room is limited.

Pets: It depends on the boat owner/charter business.

Price Range (approx. per night): Extremely variable, ranging from €100+ for a basic boat stay to €1000s for luxury yacht charters.

Address: ACI Marina Trogir, Put Cumbrijana 22, 21220 Trogir.

Booking Tips: Best Places to Stay and Finding Deals

Best Areas:

Old Town: For those who enjoy history and being at the center of it all (may be noisy in the summer).

Čiovo (near bridge or Okrug Gornji) offers beach access, greater space, and pools.

Mainland (near Old Town): Good for low-cost alternatives and convenient access to the bus station/market.

Finding Deals:

Book Off-season: Spring and autumn provide the ideal combination of pleasant weather and reduced pricing.

Book in advance, especially during the summer.

Be Flexible with Dates: Shifting your dates by a day or two can make a difference.

Look for "Genius" discounts (Booking.com) or Member Pricing if you travel frequently.

Consider Package Deals: Flights and accommodations can often be less expensive together.

Contact Property Directly: Longer stays may allow you to negotiate a better deal.

Wrapping Up

Regardless of your preferences, Trogir has a friendly site for you!

Chapter 10

SHOPPING GUIDE: SOUVENIRS, LOCAL CRAFTS, AND MORE.

While Trogir is not a major shopping destination, it does offer some great possibilities to find unique Croatian items, such as fragrant lavender and beautiful lacework. Here, quality reigns supreme above quantity.

GENUINE CROATIAN SOUVENIRS: LAVENDER, OLIVE OIL, AND LACE

Forget the usual tourist stuff; let us locate something authentically Croatian!

Lavender: Dalmatia's signature aroma! There are sachets, essential oils, soaps, and even lavender-infused honey. It's an ideal, aromatic remembrance of your journey.

Olive Oil: Croatian olive oil is of exceptional quality. Look for small, local manufacturers who offer extra virgin olive oil, maybe in an attractively wrapped bottle.

Lace (Čipka): Croatian UNESCO-recognized lace traditions include Pag lace from the island of Pag and Lepoglava lace. You might be able to locate some stunning, complicated items in specialised shops. It is a delicate and valuable art form.

Rakija: A little bottle of locally produced fruit brandy is an excellent (and powerful!) keepsake.

ARTISAN SHOPS AND GALLERIES

Wandering around the Old Town streets, you'll come across delightful small shops owned by local artists and crafters. You may find one-of-a-kind handmade pottery, paintings inspired by the Trogir backdrop, whimsical sculptures, or handcrafted leather products. These are the places where you can find a one-of-a-kind artwork while directly supporting local artists. These small treasures are something I constantly make a point of browsing.

Trogir Market (Pazar): Fresh produce and local products

The Pazar, located on the mainland immediately across the bridge, is a sensory delight and an excellent place to pick up tasty souvenirs. Along with fresh fruits and vegetables, you'll find vendors offering local honey, homemade jams, dried figs, local cheeses, and, on occasion, homemade olive oil or wine straight from the farmers. Even if you're simply browsing, you'll have a lively, real experience.

Jewelry Shops: Traditional Filigree and Coral

Trogir has a strong history of goldsmithing. Look for shops that sell stunning silver filigree jewelry, sometimes with complex, traditional Dalmatian motifs. Another Adriatic specialty is red coral jewelry, which is said to bring good luck. These items make for exquisite and lasting souvenirs. Take your time browsing and perhaps you'll find something that speaks to you.

Fashion Boutiques and Croatian Designs

While Trogir is not a high-fashion destination, it does have a few small stores that sell apparel by Croatian designers or offer one-of-a-kind resort wear, generally made of linen. You may come across a fashionable beach cover-up or a one-of-a-kind garment. If you're searching for something different from the standard high-street cuisine, stop by these shops.

Places to Buy Wine and Local Delicacies

Beyond the Pazar, seek for specialist delicatessen shops (delikatese) and wine shops (vinoteka) in the Old Town. You can discover a selected variety of Croatian wines, olive oils, truffle items (Istria, another Croatian area, is famous for them), fig pastries (smokvenjak), and other gourmet delicacies here. Staff members at these shops are often informed and can assist you in making your selection. Perfect for bringing a taste of Croatia home with you or for a delightful picnic!

Wrapping Up

Taking a small piece of Trogir home with you — or at least get some unique reminders of your trip is one of the ways we can all help keep this lovely place special for ages to come.

Chapter 11

ECOTOURISM & SUSTAINABLE TRAVEL IN TROGIR

Trogir is a treasure, and as tourists, we all play a role in preserving its beauty and distinct character for future generations. Travelling responsibly is more than just a phrase; it is about making deliberate decisions.

PRESERVING TROGIR'S UNESCO HERITAGE

This lovely Old Town has been designated a UNESCO World Heritage site for a reason. Let us treat it with the care that it deserves.

Stay On Designated Paths: Especially in historic locations, to prevent harming antique masonry.

Avoid Touching or Climbing on Monuments: It may appear apparent, yet those stones are delicate.

Be Mindful of Noise Levels: Keep in mind that people are living in Old Town, particularly in residential areas.

Dress Appropriately When Visiting Holy Sites: Provide protection for your shoulders and knees.

SUPPORTING LOCAL AND SUSTAINABLE BUSINESSES

Tourist euros can make a significant impact.

Eat At Independently Run Konobas and Restaurants: This directly benefits the local community.

Buy souvenirs from local craftsmen and producers rather than mass-produced items.

Choose Lodgings with Sustainable Practices: Find places that talk about conservation of water or renewable energy sources.

Hire Local Guides: because they offer excellent information and keep your money in the community.

Respecting Marine Life and Coastal Ecosystems.

Let's maintain the Adriatic as lovely as it is.

While swimming or snorkeling, do not touch or disturb marine creatures. Maintain a reasonable distance when observing.

Do not stand on coral or fragile seafloor regions.

Never trash on the beach or toss anything into the water. The golden guideline is to "leave no trace".

If possible, use sunscreen that is reef-safe. Some chemicals in conventional sunscreen can affect marine habitats.

Eco-friendly Activities: Kayaking, Hiking, and Cycling

These activities have no adverse effects on the environment and allow you to see Trogir's beautiful scenery up close.

Kayaking Or Paddleboarding: A relaxing way to enjoy the shore without noise or pollution.

Hiking And Cycling: Are ideal for exploring Čiovo's paths and the Pantan Nature Reserve.

Sailing (wind-powered): A beautifully sustainable method to explore the islands.

REDUCING YOUR FOOTPRINT: WASTE MANAGEMENT AND WATER CONSERVATION.

Small acts accumulate.

Bring A Reusable Water Bottle; tap water in Trogir is typically safe to drink. Refilling your bottle helps to decrease plastic waste.

Say No to Plastic Bags: by bringing your own reusable shopping bag.

Dispose Of Waste Responsibly: Use the marked bins to dispose of your rubbish responsibly. Recycle wherever feasible (Croatia is expanding its recycling infrastructure).

Conserve Water: Be mindful of your water use in hotels and flats, especially during the dry summer months. Short baths are beneficial!

Visit the Pantan Nature Reserve Responsibly

This little marsh paradise has a unique character.

To prevent harming wildlife habitats, stick to well defined pathways.

Keep the noise down, especially if you're birding.

Do not feed the animals.

Take all of the trash home with you.

Wrapping Up

By being mindful and making deliberate decisions, we can all help to keep Trogir as the magnificent, dynamic, and historically rich location that we've all grown to adore. It's about appreciating and conserving this amazing environment.

Chapter 12

UNFORGETTABLE DAY TRIPS FROM TROGIR

Would you like a change of scenery? These day trips are all reasonably straightforward to do from Trogir and offer a beautiful glimpse of the region's unique scenery, ranging from historic Roman towns to stunning national parks.

Important notes:

Travel Times: Are estimated and can vary depending on traffic, particularly during the summer.

Entry fees: Are estimates that can vary. Check official websites for the most up-to-date prices, operating hours, and seasonal changes. Adults, students, and children's prices often differ.

Special Entry Requirements:

Pets: In general, pets are not permitted within most historical sites, museums, or national park core zones (such as the waterfalls in Krka, however they may be permitted on some paths on a leash - always check park restrictions). Service animals are frequently the exception.

Alcohol and smoking: are not permitted within museums, historical sites, or sensitive nature regions. Designated smoking locations may be accessible outside.

Dress Code: For religious buildings, like as cathedrals in Split or Šibenik, modest clothes (shoulders and knees covered) is appropriate and occasionally compulsory.

SPLIT: DIOCLETIAN'S PALACE AND ROMAN HERITAGE (30 MINUTES DISTANT).

Why Go: Split, Croatia's second-largest city, is dynamic and home to the stunning Diocletian's Palace, a UNESCO World Heritage site. This isn't just ruins; it's a thriving city behind ancient Roman walls, complete with stores, cafés, and residences. Wander the Peristyle, explore the vaults, and climb the bell tower of St. Domnius Cathedral for breathtaking vistas.

Location: Split's city center.

Address: The address for Diocletian's Palace is Peristil ul., 21000, Split.

Cost of Entry (approx.): Walking around the palace grounds is free.

The Cathedral of St. Domnius and Bell Tower cost around €7-€10.

Palace Cellars (Podrumi) costs around €5-€7.

Temple of Jupiter costs around €2-€3.

Combined tickets are often available.

Getting There: Frequent busses (No. 37 from Trogir bus station), taxi/ride-sharing, or the Bura Line boat.

KRKA NATIONAL PARK: WATERFALLS AND NATURAL BEAUTY (ONE HOUR DISTANT)

Why Go: A breathtaking natural paradise famous for its flowing waterfalls, particularly Skradinski Buk. Explore the blue lake on wooden walks, visit the Franciscan monastery on Visovac Island, or see the Roški Slap waterfall by boat.

Swimming in Skradinski Buk is no longer permitted to protect the travertine formations.

Location: Near Šibenik, with primary gates in Lozovac and Skradin.

Address (Main Entrance): Lozovac b.b., 22221, Lozovac.

Cost of Entry (approximate, varies by season):

Summer (June-September): Around €40 per adult.

Shoulder Season (April-May and October): ~€20-€30.

Winter (November-March): around €7-€10.

The price covers boat transportation from Skradin to Skradinski Buk if you arrive through Skradin.

Getting There: Organized trips from Trogir, vehicle rental, or intercity bus to Šibenik, followed by local bus/taxi.

ŠIBENIK: ST. JAMES CATHEDRAL AND HISTORIC FORTS (ONE HOUR AWAY)

Why go: A picturesque medieval city, less congested than Split, with its own UNESCO World Heritage Site: The

Cathedral of St. James (Katedrala Sv. Jakova), a one-of-a-kind masterpiece of Renaissance architecture constructed entirely of stone. Explore its historic old town and climb to one of its outstanding fortifications (such as St. Michael's or Barone) to enjoy panoramic views.

Location: Šibenik city center.

Address: Trg Republike Hrvatske 1, 22000, Šibenik.

Cost Of Entry (Approx.):

St. James Cathedral costs around €5-€7.

St. Michael's Fortress and Barone Fortress costs between €10 and €15. A combo ticket is often available.

Getting There: Take an intercity bus from Trogir or rent a vehicle.

SALONA: THE RUINS OF AN ANCIENT ROMAN CITY (20 MINUTES AWAY)

Why go: Salona, located just a short distance from Trogir, was once the thriving capital of the Roman province of Dalmatia and one of the greatest towns in the Roman empire. Today, it is a large archeological site with remarkable remnants of an amphitheater, basilicas, baths, and city walls. It's intriguing to explore and picture its previous magnificence. Much less congested than other locations.

Location: Solin is a town situated outside of Split, near Trogir.

Address (Archaeological Park): Put Salone BB, 21210 Solin.

Entry costs around €5-€8.

Getting There: Take a short cab or ride-share, a local bus to Split (ask for the Salona station), or rent a vehicle.

PRIMOŠTEN: A PICTURESQUE COASTAL TOWN (45 MINUTES DISTANT)

Why Go: One of the most picturesque small settlements along the Dalmatian coast. Primošten's ancient town is located on a small peninsula connected to the mainland by a thin causeway, with a large church at the highest point. It's famous for its lovely beaches (like Raduča) and the surrounding Bucavac wineries, which have distinctive stone-walled plots. Ideal for a leisurely day of swimming and walking.

Location: Primošten is located along the beach route connecting Trogir and Šibenik.

Directions (Old Town): Follow signs to Primošten Center.

Cost of entry: Free to explore the town and beaches. Parking costs apply.

Getting There: Rent a vehicle (most scenic) or take an intercity bus.

INLAND DALMATIA: EXPLORING ZAGORA REGION

Why Go: For a completely different experience of Dalmatia, travel inland to the Zagora area. This is a more rocky, rural terrain, with small towns, stone cottages, vineyards, and olive trees. It is less touristy and gives a look into traditional Croatian life. You may stop by a local agroturismo for a genuine dinner, explore the source of the Cetina River (near Vrlika), or visit the old town of Sinj, which is famous for its Alka knight tournament.

Location: The area inland from the shore, north/northeast of Trogir.

Entry Fee: The cost of entry varies depending on the activity.

Getting There: For optimum freedom, rent a vehicle and explore. Tours may be arranged for certain places.

Wrapping Up

Day tours offer an excellent opportunity to enhance your stay in Trogir. Choose one or two that spark your attention, and you'll get a greater appreciation for Dalmatia's splendor and diversity!

Chapter 13

CURATED ITINERARIES FOR EVERY TRAVELER

Whether you have one day or a week, here are some ideas to help you make the most of your Trogir vacation.

TROGIR IN A DAY: THE WHIRLWIND TOUR

Goal: Visit the Old Town's must-see attractions.

Morning (9 a.m. to 12 p.m.)

Arrive and go straight to the Old Town. Enter via the Land Gate

Explore St. Lawrence Cathedral; do not skip Radovan's Portal and climb the Bell Tower for breathtaking views.

Wander around the main plaza, enjoying the Town Loggia and Clock Tower.

Afternoon (12 PM–5 PM):

Lunch at a konoba in the old town.

Visit the Kamerlengo Fortress and walk its ramparts.

Stroll down the Riva promenade, taking in the ambiance.

A quick visit to the Cipiko Palaces (outside) and Sea Gate.

Evening (5 p.m. onward):

Have an early dinner on the Riva or pick a location for a sunset cocktail viewing the harbour.

Before going, take one more stroll around the lit Old Town.

PERFECT WEEKEND IN TROGIR (2-3 DAYS)

Goal: Immerse yourself in the Old Town and explore Čiovo.

Day 1: Old Town Immersion

Follow the morning agenda for "Trogir in a Day."

Lunch comes in the afternoon. Explore the Trogir Town Museum. Explore the quieter northern lanes for secret courtyards.

Dinner in a quaint Old Town restaurant. If live music is available, enjoy it.

Day 2: Čiovo, Relaxation and Culture

Visit the Benedictine Monastery of St. Nicholas (Kairos Collection). Tour the local Pazar (market) on the mainland.

Afternoon: Visit Čiovo Island. Relax on a beach like Okrug Gornji (Copacabana), or seek out a calmer cove. Swimming and sunbathing are enjoyable activities.

Evening: Activities include sunset cocktails on Čiovo overlooking Trogir, followed by dinner at a coastal restaurant nearby or downtown Trogir.

(Optional Day 3): Day trip or further dive.

Option A (Day Trip): Take a quick trip to Split to view Diocletian's Palace or explore the Salona ruins.

Option B (Trogir): Return to a favorite site, take a short boat trip (for example, to the Blue Lagoon if time permits), or explore Marmont's Gloriette.

HISTORY BUFF'S ITINERARY (3-4 DAYS)

Goal: Explore every historical nook and crevice.

Day 1 and 2: Follow the "Perfect Weekend" plan, making sure to see St. Lawrence Cathedral, Kamerlengo, the Town Museum, Cipiko Palaces, both Town Gates, St. Nicholas Monastery, and St. Dominic's Church.

Day 3: Roman roots and lesser-known sites.

Morning: Day trip to Salona to explore the huge Roman remains.

Afternoon: Head back to Trogir. Look for smaller churches such as St. Barbara and St. Peter. Investigate Marmont's Gloriette.

Dinner: Perhaps look for a restaurant in a historic structure.

Day 4: Regional Historical Context

Morning: Trip to Šibenik to visit St. James Cathedral and its medieval forts.

Afternoon: Continue exploring Šibenik or return to Trogir for a last walk, maybe focusing on architectural elements overlooked.

Evening: Farewell dinner and reflection on centuries of history.

THE BEACH LOVERS AND ADVENTURER'S ITINERARY (5-7 DAYS)

Goal: Combine Old Town beauty with lots of sun, sea, and exciting activities.

Day 1: The fundamentals of Old Town (Cathedral, Kamerlengo, and Riva).

Day 2: Čiovo Beach Day with Water Sports

Morning/Afternoon: Visit Okrug Gornji. Rent a jet ski, go paddleboarding, or simply relax on the beach.

Evening: Experience sunset at the beach bar and a relaxed dinner on Čiovo.

Day 3: Island Hopping Boat Trip.

Full-day boat tour to the Blue Lagoon, Šolta, and/or Drvenik Islands. Swimming, snorkeling, and exploring.

Day 4 - Active Exploration

Morning: Rent a scooter or bicycle to explore hidden coves and beaches on Čiovo.

Afternoon: Go kayaking along the shore or take a diving taster.

Evening: Relaxed dinner, maybe a grill if your accommodations permit.

Day 5: Adventure at Krka National Park

Full-day trip to Krka National Park for waterfalls and environmental hikes.

Day 6 (optional): Mainland Hiking/Cycling or Additional Water Fun

Explore hiking routes on iovo or the mainland, or enjoy your favorite water activity on another day.

Day 7: Relax, explore favorite sites, and go shopping for souvenirs.

A Relaxed Pace: Trogir for Slow Travellers (7+ Days)

Goal: Take it everything in, live like a native, and fully relax.

Days 1-3: Gently explore the Old Town's highlights, one or two every day. Spend a lot of time people-watching in cafés on Riva. Visit the Pazar bazaar at your leisure.

Days 4-5: Spend time with Čiovo. Find your favorite secluded beach. Take time to read a book. Take extended meals at the seashore konobas.

Day 6: Consider participating in a cultural immersion activity such as a local cooking lesson or an olive oil tasting.

Day 7: Enjoy a leisurely day trip, such as a boat trip to Slatine or a slow exploration of Primošten.

Ongoing: Return to places you once loved. Spend your mornings exploring with no agenda. Enjoy lengthy, leisurely dinners. Perhaps learn a few additional Croatian words and converse with the locals. Find your favorite pekara (bakery) for morning pastries.

FAMILY FUN: A KID-FRIENDLY TROGIR ITINERARY (CUSTOMIZE DURATION AS NEEDED)

Goal: Keep the kids (and teenagers!) amused while experiencing Trogir's charm.

Daily Structure: Combine sightseeing with leisure activities and relaxation.

Morning:

Explore Kamerlengo Fortress (children adore climbing the ramparts!).

Scavenger quest in the Old Town (search for stone lions and special sculptures).

Visit the Pazar market, which is colorful and intriguing.

Afternoon

Beach activities in Čiovo (Okrug Gornji offers better amenities and calmer seas).

Boat trip to the Blue Lagoon (popular activities include swimming and snorkeling).

Ice cream break on the Riva.

Consider visiting a neighboring water park, such as Solaris Aquapark in Šibenik, for a day trip.

Evening

Casual family dinners (pizzerias are usually an excellent choice).

Stroll down the Riva and keep an eye out for boats.

Look for outdoor entertainment or street performers (seasonal).

Marmont's Gloriette can be an enjoyable place for children to romp around.

Wrapping Up

Remember that these are simply frameworks. The best itinerary for Trogir is one that makes you happy! Enjoy!

CHAPTER 14

TROGIR FOR FAMILIES: ADVENTURES WITH KIDS

Let's have a look at how to keep everyone happy and involved in this lovely part of Croatia, from infants to teenagers. My kids have loved our Trogir trips, and I'm sure yours will as well!

Important Notes for Families:

Costs: For extremely young children, entry prices for kids are frequently lowered or free. Always check particular age groups.

Strollers/Prams: The Old Town's cobblestones can be uneven. A sturdy stroller or baby carrier is recommended for little children.

Sun Protection: essential for fragile skin! Hats, sunscreen, and rash vests are your best companions.

Hydration: Keep your water bottles topped up, especially in the heat.

BEST KID-FRIENDLY ATTRACTIONS AND SIGHTS

✓ Kamerlengo Fortress (Old Town)

Why Kids Love It: It is a genuine castle! They can climb the walls, look through arrow holes, and imagine knights and battles. The views are a treat for parents.

Location: The location is on the southwestern point of the Trogir Old Town island.

Address: Obala Bana Berislavića, 21220, Trogir.

Entry Fee: Around €4-€5 for adults, and typically less for children.

Special Entry Requirements: Hold onto little children's hands on the ramparts; some drops are substantial. There are no pets inside.

✓ **Riva Promenade (Old Town**

Why Kids Love It: There's plenty of room to run (carefully!), boating, ice cream parlors, and, in the summer, street entertainers or painters.

Location: On the southern end of the Old Town island.

There is no entry fee.

Special Entry Requirements: Keep a watch on kids near the water's edge.

✓ **Trogir Old Town "Scavenger Hunt"**

Why Kids Love It: It makes touring into a game! Before you go, compile a list of items to look for, such as a stone lion, a certain coat of arms, Radovan's Adam and Eve, a well, and a sleeping cat.

Location: Throughout Old Town.

There is no entry fee.

✓ **Marmont's Gloriette (Oldtown)**

Why Kids Love It: This little neoclassical monument on the western point gives some open area for a brief run-around and a unique perspective of the sea.

Location: At the western extremity of Trogir's Old Town island, between Kamerlengo and St. Mark's Tower.

There is no entry fee.

Best Beaches for Families: Shallow Waters and Amenities

✓ Okrug Gornji Beach ("Copacabana"), Čiovo Island.

Why Families Love It: Long pebble beach, reasonably shallow entrance in certain areas, and a variety of services such as sunbed and umbrella rentals, cafés, ice cream, inflatable water parks (seasonal), and water sports.

Location: Okrug Gornji on Čiovo Island.

Cost: There is no charge to visit the beach. Prices for rentals and activities.

Getting there: By water taxi from Trogir Riva, local bus, or automobile.

✓ Slatine Beaches, Čiovo Island

Why Families Love It: It's often calmer than Okrug Gornji, and there are several little pebble coves. Often suitable for families wanting a more relaxed atmosphere. Some coves have extremely mild slopes into the water.

Location: The village of Slatine is located in the eastern section of Čiovo island.

Entry Fee: The cost of entry is free. There are fewer amenities than Okrug Gornji, so pack appropriately.

Getting There: Local buses, cars, and occasionally water taxis.

✓ **Pantan Beach (Mainland, near the Pantan Nature Reserve)**

Why families love it: A mixture of sand and pebbles, generally shallower and calmer owing to the river mouth. Close to the natural reserve for some exploring.

Location: East of Trogir on the mainland.

The cost of entry is free. Basic facilities.

Getting there: Short drive/taxi or longer walk/cycle.

Activities Kids Will Enjoy: Boat Trips and Water Parks (Nearby)

Boat trip to the Blue Lagoon (Krknjaši Bay).

Why Children Enjoy It: The boat voyage itself is an experience! The crystal-clear turquoise water is ideal for swimming and snorkeling (bring kids' gear!). Several excursions include lunch.

Departure point: Trogir Riva.

Cost (approx.): Half/full day trips typically cost between €30 and €60 per person.

Special Entry Requirements: Ensure that life jackets are accessible and suitable for minors.

✓ **Solaris Aquapark In Šibenik For a Day Vacation.**

Why Children Love It: A full-fledged water park with slides, pools, and lazy rivers. A surefire hit if you're looking for a day excursion.

Location: Solaris Beach Resort is located in Šibenik, approximately an hour's drive from Trogir.

Address: Hoteli Solaris 86, 22000 Šibenik.

Cost of Entry: €20-€30 per person (about) (can vary by height/age).

Special Entry Requirements: The standard water park restrictions apply.

✓ **Semi-submarine Tour (from Trogir Riva)**

Why Children Love It: Provides a view underwater without getting wet! The bottom of the boat features windows that allow you to observe the fish and seafloor. Younger kids benefit from short outings.

Departure: Trogir Riva (seasonal).

Cost is around €10-€15 per person.

DINING OUT WITH KIDS: FAMILY-FRIENDLY RESTAURANTS

Pizzerias are always a safe bet! Many in Trogir Old Town and Čiovo.

Konoba Trs (Old Town): Although a respected konoba, they are frequently accommodating to families and have a nice courtyard.

Address: Matije Gupca 14.

Riva restaurants: Many offer kids' servings or basic pasta/grill meals. The view keeps everyone entertained.

Tip: Most Croatian restaurants are family-friendly. Don't hesitate to request simpler preparations or lesser amounts.

PLAYGROUNDS AND RECREATION AREAS

Čiovo has a small public playground near the major beach and harbor area.

The Riva: offers open spaces. The landscape around Marmont's Gloriette is very nice.

Mainland Parks: If you're staying in mainland Trogir, there may be additional local neighborhood parks available. Inquire with your lodging host for local recommendations.

Wrapping Up

With a little forethought, Trogir can be a terrific excursion for the entire family, leaving memories that will last long after the ice cream has gone!

Chapter 15

TROGIR AFTER DARK: EVENING ENTERTAINMENT, NIGHTLIFE

As the sun sinks below the horizon, coloring the sky in flaming hues, Trogir takes on a new kind of charm. The old stones shimmer under mild lighting, and a comfortable, sociable attitude pervades the air. It is hardly a rowdy party town, but it does have plenty to offer for a fantastic evening.

SUNSET VIEWS WITH COCKTAIL BARS

Watching the sunset is nearly a daily routine here, and with good cause!

Kamerlengo Fortress: While it may close before real dark, the views from here as the sun begins to drop are breathtaking.

Riva Promenade: Take a seat at one of the many cafés and bars along the Riva. Many places provide comfortable sitting to have a beverage while viewing the sunset over the water and Čiovo. Caffe Bar Smokvica and Focus Bar are popular destinations.

Bars on Čiovo (Okrug Gornji): Beach bars, such as Laganini Beach Club (seasonal) or others along Copacabana, offer stunning sunset views towards the mainland.

Location: Locations vary along Trogir Riva and Čiovo waterfronts.

Drink prices range between ~€7-€12.

Special Entry Requirements: Generally relaxed, however certain trendier establishments may have a somewhat sharper casual dress code in the evenings.

Live Music: Klapa Singing, Local Bands

Hearing music in Trogir's historic surroundings has a powerful emotional impact.

Klapa Singing: Keep an ear out for klapa (traditional Dalmatian acapella harmony singing) performances, whether they are spontaneous or scheduled. Groups can practice or present in courtyards, the Town Loggia, and even restaurants. It is eerily gorgeous.

Local Bands: During the summer, many restaurants and bars, particularly those along the Riva or in Old Town squares, provide live music, which often includes performances by acoustic duos, local bands singing covers, or traditional Dalmatian music.

Locations: Often promoted on posters, or simply follow your ears! Check the Trogir Tourist Board for event calendars.

Cost: Typically, free in public areas or with a drink/meal at a venue.

THE RIVA PROMENADE AT NIGHT: STROLLING AND SOCIALIZING

The Riva is the center of Trogir's nightly social scene.

Why It's Special: After dinner, both locals and guests take a leisurely passeggiata (stroll) along the waterfront. It is bustling with conversations, laughter, clinking glasses, and the soft rolling of waves against the moored boats. The Old Town and Kamerlengo Fortress are brilliantly lit.

Location: Trogir Riva.

Cost: Free (unless you want more ice cream!).

There are no special entry requirements; simply enjoy the bright and pleasant atmosphere.

LATE-NIGHT BARS AND BEACH CLUBS (SEASONAL)

While Trogir is more about romantic evenings than all-night raves, there are possibilities for continuing your night.

Old Town Bars: Some small bars nestled away in Old Town alleys stay open longer, giving a comfortable setting for a late drink.

Beach Clubs in Čiovo (e.g., Okrug Gornji): During peak summer, certain beach bars transform into vibrant club-like establishments with DJs and dancing, especially on weekends. Laganini Beach Club and comparable places frequently organize parties.

Locations: Scattered, Čiovo offering beach clubs.

Cost: Drink pricing. Cover charges may apply to special events at clubs.

Special Entry Requirements: Clubs may have an age limit (18+) and a dress code (smart casual).

Cultural Events and Outdoor Performances.

Summer in Trogir is frequently filled with cultural events.

Trogir Cultural Summer: This event takes place from June to September and has a broad schedule of classical music concerts, folklore performances, theatrical productions, and art exhibitions, which are frequently hosted in spectacular open-air sites such as the Kamerlengo Fortress courtyard or town squares.

Kamerlengo Fortress occasionally offers open-air cinema.

Locations: Schedules and locations can be found on the Trogir Tourist Board website or on posters throughout town.

Cost varies; some events are free, while others need a ticket (often between €10 and €30+).

Special entry requirements vary depending on the event.

Wrapping Up

Trogir after dark is all about soaking up the ambiance, spending time with friends, and being enchanted by the splendor of the lit town. Whether it's a calm drink, wonderful music, or a boisterous conversation on the Riva, your nights here will be unforgettable.

Chapter 16

ESSENTIAL DOS AND DON'TS FOR RESPECTFUL AND SAFE TRAVEL IN TROGIR

Consider this a friendly guide to handling social situations and local traditions in Trogir. It's not about following strict regulations, but rather about being mindful and respectful, which, in my experience, always leads to more enjoyable travel experiences.

CULTURAL ETIQUETTE: RESPECT FOR LOCAL CUSTOMS

Croatians, particularly those in Dalmatia, place a high value on politeness, family, and a generally laid-back attitude toward life. Here are some pointers.

Greetings: Simply saying "Dobar dan" (Good day) when entering a shop or small café, or "Dovidenja" (Goodbye) when leaving, can go a long way. When meeting someone for the first time, a handshake is common. Direct eye contact during a conversation is normal and indicates engagement.

Patience Is a Virtue: Things may move at a bit slower pace than you are accustomed to, particularly in smaller places or during high season. Embrace the pomalo philosophy. Getting flustered will not speed things up and may cause unneeded tension for everyone. Relax, you're on vacation!

Respect for Elders: Older folks are often treated with a lot of respect. It is a great gesture to offer a seat on a bus to an old person who is standing, for example.

Invitations: It's normal to bring a small gift, such as a bottle of wine, chocolates, or flowers for the hostess, if you're fortunate enough to be asked into a local's home (which can happen because Croatians are welcoming!). Accept any gift of food or drink; it is a gesture of welcome.

Sensitive Themes: While Croatians are typically open, it's definitely best to avoid excessively sensitive historical or political subjects, particularly those relating to the 1990s wars, unless you know someone well and they bring them up first.

Public Demeanor: While Trogir is a tourist destination, excessively loud or rowdy conduct in public, particularly away from beach bars, may be frowned upon. Respect the tranquility in residential neighborhoods, especially at night.

Do: Try Local Food, Learn Basic Phrases, Be Patient

These are my golden principles for anyplace I visit, and they absolutely apply in Trogir!

DO Try Local Food: Please, please, please explore beyond pizza and bland tourist cuisine! Dalmatian food is amazing. Be adventurous. Ask for suggestions. Sample the peka, pašticada, fresh grilled seafood, local cheeses, and olive oil. It is such an important part of the culture.

DO Learn Basic Phrases: You don't have to be fluent, but knowing a few basic Croatian words will be greatly appreciated and can lead to opportunities.

Dobar Dan (DOH-bahr Dahn): Good day

Hvala (HVAH-lah): Thank you.

Molim (MOH-leem): Please / You're welcome.

Da (dah): Yes.

Ne (neh): No

Excuse me/Sorry (oh-PROHS-tee-teh).

Even a clumsy attempt usually brings a smile!

DO Be Patient: I mentioned this before, but it is worth repeating. Service may be relaxed, and lineups may occur. Take a deep breath, enjoy the sunshine, and remember you are not hurrying to catch a train.

Don't: Dress Inappropriately at Religious Sites; Bargain Excessively

Here is some crucial "don'ts" to bear in mind:

DON'T Dress Inappropriately for Religious Sites: When exploring churches such as St. Lawrence Cathedral or any other religious building, it is customary to dress modestly. If you're dressed for the beach, keep a light scarf or sarong in your bag for easy coverage when needed. Walking into a church in your swimsuit is an absolute no-no.

Don't haggle Aggressively (except maybe lightly at open-air markets): Haggling is not a common practice in Croatia in shops or restaurants. Prices are usually fixed. At the Pazar (open-air market), you could get a small reduction if you're buying many items, but aggressive bargaining will likely be met with dissatisfaction. A polite inquiry about a "much better offer" is basically as far as it often goes.

TIPPING CULTURE IN CROATIA

Tipping is common in Croatia, but it's probably not as established or as high percentage-wise as in some other nations (like the US).

Restaurants and Cafes: If you're pleased with the service, leaving an extra 5-10% is a kind gesture that is usually appreciated. If service is included (check the bill), an extra tip is not required but is appreciated for good service. Even if you pay the bill with a credit card, it is common to leave the tip in cash.

Bars: For beverages, round up to the next convenient amount or leave some loose cash.

Taxis: Rounding up the fare is common.

Tour Guides: If you had an excellent tour, a 10% tip or a predetermined amount (€5-€10 per person for a good half-day trip, for example) is a lovely way to express gratitude.

Hotel Staff: A small tip (€1-€2) is welcomed but not often demanded for porters and housekeepers.

Essentially, tip if you believe the service is worth it, but do not feel compelled to do so.

Environmental Responsibility: Leave No Trace

This is related to our eco-tourism chapter, but it is so vital that it deserves to be mentioned again. Trogir's splendor is precious.

DON'T Litter: Ever. Anywhere. Use containers or carry your garbage with you until you locate one. This includes cigarette butts!

DO Respect Nature: Stay on walkways, don't pick wildflowers in protected areas, and don't disturb wildlife.

DO Be Water Wise: Water is a valuable resource, especially in summer. Be cautious of your usage.

DO Reduce Plastic Use: Bring a water bottle that is reusable and shopping bag.

Wrapping Up

Following these basic do's and don'ts will not only show respect for Trogir and its people, but will also improve your personal experience by encouraging nice encounters and leaving with even fonder memories. It's all about being a mindful and responsible traveler!

Chapter 17

LOCAL LINGO: USEFUL CROATIAN PHRASES & SLANG

Let's arm you with some essential Croatian to navigate Trogir like a charm. I've broken it down into handy categories.

BASIC GREETINGS & COURTESIES

(These are your everyday magic words!)

Dobar dan (DOH-bahr dahn): Good day (general greeting during the day)

Dobro jutro (DOH-broh YOO-troh): Good morning

Dobra večer (DOH-brah VEH-chehr): Good evening

Laku noć (LAH-koo notch): Good night (when leaving or going to bed)

Bok (bohk): Hi / Bye (informal, very common)

Doviđenja (doh-vee-JEH-nyah): Goodbye (more formal)

Hvala (HVAH-lah): Thank you

Hvala lijepa (HVAH-lah LYEE-pah)": Thank you very much (literally "thank you beautifully")

Molim (MOH-leem): Please / You're welcome / Excuse me (when trying to get attention)

Oprostite (oh-PROHS-tee-teh): Excuse me / Sorry (for bumping into someone, or to get attention)

Kako ste? (KAH-koh steh?): How are you? (formal)

Kako si? (KAH-koh see?): How are you? (informal)

Dobro sam, hvala. (DOH-broh sahm, HVAH-lah.): I'm fine, thank you.

Drago mi je. (DRAH-goh mee yeh.): Pleased to meet you.

Da (dah): Yes

Ne (neh): No

Možda (MOHZH-dah): Maybe

Nema na čemu (NEH-mah nah CHEH-moo): You're welcome (in response to "Hvala")

Ugodan dan! (OO-goh-dahn dahn!) - Have a pleasant day!

Govorite li engleski? (goh-VOH-ree-teh lee EN-gless-kee?) - Do you speak English?

ORDERING FOOD AND DRINKS: USEFUL PHRASES

Ja bih... (yah bih...): I would like... (polite)

Htio/Htjela bih... (HTEE-oh / HTYEH-lah bih...): I would like... (Htio for male speaker, Htjela for female)

Molim vas, jelovnik. (MOH-leem vahs, YEH-lohv-neek.): The menu, please.

Što preporučujete? (SHTOH preh-poh-roo-CHOO-yeh-teh?): What do you recommend?

Jedno pivo, molim. (YEHD-noh PEE-voh, MOH-leem.): One beer, please.

Čašu vina, molim. (CHAH-shoo VEE-nah, MOH-leem.): A glass of wine, please. (Bijelo - white, Crno - red)

Vodu, molim. (VOH-doo, MOH-leem.): Water, please. (Običnu - still, Mineralnu/Gaziranu - sparkling)

Kavu, molim. (KAH-voo, MOH-leem.): Coffee, please. (S mlijekom - with milk, Bez mlijeka - without milk)

Račun, molim. (RAH-choon, MOH-leem.): The bill, please.

Je li ovo slobodno? (yeh lee OH-voh SLOH-boh-dnoh?): Is this (table/seat) free?

Jako je ukusno! (YAH-koh yeh OO-koos-noh!): It's very tasty!

Imate li...? (EE-mah-teh lee...?): Do you have...?

Bez leda, molim. (Bez LEH-dah, MOH-leem.): Without ice, please.

Još jedno, molim. (yosh YEHD-noh, MOH-leem.): Another one, please.

Za ovdje ili za ponijeti? (zah OHV-dyeh EE-lee zah POH-nyeh-tee?): For here or to take away?

Mogu li dobiti...? (MOH-goo lee DOH-bee-tee...?): Can I get/have...?

Što je ovo? (SHTOH yeh OH-voh?): What is this?

Živjeli! (ZHEE-vyeh-lee!): Cheers!

ASKING FOR DIRECTIONS: GETTING AROUND

Oprostite, gdje je...? (oh-PROHS-tee-teh, GDYEH yeh...?): Excuse me, where is...?

...katedrala? (...kah-teh-DRAH-lah?): ...the cathedral?

...plaža? (...PLAH-zhah?): the beach?

...autobusni kolodvor? (...ow-toh-BOOS-nee KOH-loh-dvohr?): ...the bus station?

...WC / toalet? (...veh-TSEH / TOH-ah-let?) - ...the toilet?

Lijevo (LYEH-voh) - Left

Desno (DESS-noh) - Right

Ravno (RAHV-noh) - Straight ahead

Blizu (BLEE-zoo) - Near

Daleko (dah-LEH-koh) - Far

Ovdje (OHV-dyeh) - Here

Tamo (TAH-moh) - There

Kako mogu doći do...? (KAH-koh MOH-goo DOH-chee doh...?): How can I get to...?

Hvala na pomoći. (HVAH-lah nah POH-moh-chee.): Thanks for the help.

Je li ovo pravi put za...? (yeh lee OH-voh PRAH-vee poot zah...?): Is this the right way to...?

Preko puta (PREH-koh POO-tah): Across the street

Izgubio/Izgubila sam se. (EEZ-goo-bee-oh / EEZ-goo-bee-lah sahm seh.) - I am lost. (Izgubio for male, Izgubila for female)

NUMBERS AND TIME: UNDERSTANDING CROATIAN NUMERALS

This section is crucial. I'm focusing on Croatian numbers and time-telling.)

Jedan (YEH-dahn): One

Dva (dvah): Two

Tri (tree): Three

Četiri (CHEH-tee-ree): Four

Pet (pet): Five

Šest (shest): Six

Sedam (SEH-dahm): Seven

Osam (OH-sahm): Eight

Devet (DEH-vet): Nine

Deset (DEH-set): Ten

Jedanaest (yeh-DAH-nah-est): Eleven

Dvanaest (DVAH-nah-est): Twelve

Dvadeset (DVAH-deh-set): Twenty

Pedeset (peh-DEH-set): Fifty

Sto (stoh): One hundred

Koliko je sati? (KOH-lee-koh yeh SAH-tee?): What time is it?

Jedan sat. (YEH-dahn saht.): One o'clock.

Pola dva. (POH-lah dvah.) - Half past one (literally "half two").

Petnaest do tri. (PET-nah-est doh tree.) - Quarter to three (fifteen to three).

Danas (DAH-nahs) - Today / Sutra (SOO-trah) - Tomorrow / Jučer (YOO-chehr) - Yesterday

SHOPPING: MAKING PURCHASES

Koliko ovo košta? (KOH-lee-koh OH-voh KOSH-tah?) - How much does this cost?

Mogu li ovo probati? (MOH-goo lee OH-voh PROH-bah-tee?) - Can I try this on?

Imate li ovo u drugoj boji? (EE-mah-teh lee OH-voh oo DROO-goy BOY-ee?) - Do you have this in another color?

Imate li veću/manju veličinu? (EE-mah-teh lee VEH-choo/MAH-nyoo veh-lee-CHEE-noo?) - Do you have a bigger/smaller size?

Uzet ću ovo. (OO-zet choo OH-voh.) - I'll take this.

Plaćam gotovinom. (PLAH-chahm goh-toh-VEE-nohm.) - I'm paying with cash.

Plaćam karticom. (PLAH-chahm KAR-tee-tsohm.) - I'm paying by card.

Mogu li dobiti vrećicu? (MOH-goo lee DOH-bee-tee VREH-chee-tsoo?) - Can I get a bag?

Samo gledam, hvala. (SAH-moh GLEH-dahm, HVAH-lah.) - I'm just looking, thank you.

Gdje je blagajna? (GDYEH yeh blah-GUY-nah?) - Where is the cash register?

Popust? (POH-poost?) - Discount? (Use sparingly and politely)

Račun, molim. (RAH-choon, MOH-leem.) - The receipt, please. (Same as for restaurants)

Otvoreno (OHT-voh-reh-noh) - Open

Zatvoreno (ZAHT-voh-reh-noh) - Closed

Emergency Phrases: In Case of Trouble

(Hopefully, you won't need these, but good to know!)

Upomoć! (OO-poh-mohtch!) - Help!

Zovite policiju! (ZOH-vee-teh poh-LEE-tsee-yoo!) - Call the police!

Zovite hitnu pomoć! (ZOH-vee-teh HEET-noo POH-mohtch!) - Call an ambulance!

Trebam liječnika. (TREH-bahm LYEECH-nee-kah.) - I need a doctor.

Gdje je bolnica? (GDYEH yeh BOHL-nee-tsah?) - Where is the hospital?

Gdje je ljekarna? (GDYEH yeh lyeh-KAR-nah?) - Where is the pharmacy?

Ukradeno mi je... (OO-krah-deh-noh mee yeh...) - My ... has been stolen. (...novčanik - wallet, ...torba - bag, ...putovnica - passport)

Ne osjećam se dobro. (neh OH-syeh-chahm seh DOH-broh.) - I don't feel well.

Imam bolove. (EE-mahm BOH-loh-veh.) - I have pain.

Vatra! / Požar! (VAH-trah! / POH-zhahr!) - Fire!

Pazite! (PAH-zee-teh!) - Watch out! / Be careful!

Ne govorim hrvatski. (neh GOH-voh-reem HRR-vaht-skee.) - I don't speak Croatian.

Molim vas, govorite polako. (MOH-leem vahs, goh-VOH-ree-teh poh-LAH-koh.) - Please speak slowly.

Ne razumijem. (neh rah-ZOO-myehm.) - I don't understand.

Hitni broj je 112. (HEET-nee broy yeh YEH-dahn YEH-dahn dvah.) - The emergency number is 112. (This is the universal European emergency number).

Wrapping Up

That's a lot, mastering a few from each category will make a world of difference. Good luck

Chapter 18

PRACTICAL INFORMATION AND TRAVEL TIPS.

This is where we go over the details, such as where to find tourist office, what to do if you need a medication, and how to manage your holiday money.

TOURIST INFORMATION CENTERS' LOCATIONS AND SERVICES

For queries, maps, brochures, and local event information, contact the Trogir Tourist Board (Turistička zajednica grada Trogira). They are really helpful and typically use English-speaking personnel.

Main Location: Their main office is usually located directly in the middle of the Old Town, often on or near the main plaza, Trg Ivana Pavla II, or on the Riva. Look for a "i" sign.

Services: They Can Provide You:

Maps of Trogir and its surroundings are available for free.

Brochures featuring attractions, activities, and day trips.

Information about current events, festivals, and exhibitions.

Advice about public transportation timetables.

Sometimes aid is provided in obtaining lodging (though reserving ahead of time is usually recommended).

Insider Tip: I usually make a point of stopping in when I visit a new town; they're a treasure trove of excellent, up-to-date information.

Connections: Wi-Fi Hotspots, SIM Cards, and Mobile Data

Staying connected is rather simple in Trogir.

Wi-Fi Hotspots: The majority of hotels, restaurants, and cafés offer free Wi-Fi to its customers. The Wi-Fi icon will often be displayed. The Old Town also has public Wi-Fi places; however, the connection can be poor within the thick stone walls.

SIM Cards: If you're staying for a while or need dependable data on the go, purchasing a local Croatian prepaid SIM card is an excellent choice. You can acquire them from kiosks (like Tisak or iNovine), post offices, or mobile phone carrier stores (e.g., Hrvatski Telekom/T-Mobile, A1, Telemach). They normally offer nice tourist packages with lots of data for an affordable cost (e.g., €10-€20 for a week or two of decent data). Make sure your phone is unlocked before you depart.

Mobile Data (Roaming): If you're from the EU, your home cell plan should include free roaming in Croatia ("Roam Like at Home"). Non-EU travelers should verify their home provider's roaming rates; they can be costly, making a local SIM a far better value.

HEALTH AND SAFETY: PHARMACIES, MEDICAL FACILITIES, AND EMERGENCY NUMBERS

Hopefully, you have no need for these, but it's always a good idea to know.

Pharmacies (Ljekarna): Pharmacies in Trogir are normally signposted with a green cross. They can offer over-the-counter drugs and advise on mild conditions. One is usually found on the mainland near the market/bus station, with a smaller one in the Old Town. Look for signs that read "LJEKARNA." Pharmacists are often fluent in English.

Medical Facilities (Dom Zdravlja / Bolnica): For minor concerns, Trogir has a local health facility (Dom Zdravlja) (typically on the mainland). For major cases, the primary hospital (Klinički bolnički centar Split - Firule ili Križine) is located in Split, approximately a 30--40-minute drive away. Your travel insurance policy should cover medical emergencies.

Emergency Numbers:

112: This is the single European emergency number for the police, ambulance, and fire departments. It's the most crucial thing to remember.

192: Police

193 - Fire Brigade

194: Ambulance

Financial Matters: ATMs, Banks, and Currency Exchange

Croatia uses the euro (€).

ATMs (bankomats): Widely available throughout Trogir, including the Old Town, the Riva, and the mainland. They accept the majority of foreign cards. Be aware that your home bank may charge a fee for international withdrawals, and that some ATMs (particularly non-bank ones such as Euronet) may charge greater fees or provide less advantageous exchange rates; if feasible, use ATMs affiliated to legitimate banks.

Banks (Banka): Major Croatian banks, such as Zagrebačka banka, Privredna banka Zagreb (PBZ), Erste Bank, and OTP Banka, have branches in Trogir, generally on the mainland. They offer currency exchange as well as other financial services.

Currency Exchange (Mjenjačnica): Dedicated exchange offices are available. Compare prices and seek for "no commission" signs, but always check the ultimate amount you'll receive. Exchanging at a bank is often the safest way to get decent rates. If possible, avoid exchanging money at airports or hotels because the exchange rates are typically lower.

Credit Cards: These are widely accepted in the majority of hotels, restaurants, and major shops. However, it's always a good idea to have extra cash on hand for smaller purchases, such as market stalls, cafés, and smaller konobas.

PUBLIC HOLIDAYS AND OPEN HOURS

Public Holidays: Croatia has several public holidays. On certain days, banks, post offices, and some shops may be closed or have limited hours. Major ones include:

New Years Day (January 1)

Epiphany (January 6)

Easter Sunday and Monday.

Labor Day (May 1)

Statehood Day (May 30).

Corpus Christi (movable; May/June)

Anti-fascist Struggle Day (June 22)

Victory and Homeland Thanksgiving Day (August 5).

Assumption Day (August 15)

All Saints Day (November 1)

Remembrance Day for Victims of the Homeland War (November 18)

Christmas Day (December 25) and Saint Stephen's Day (December 26)

Check a Croatian calendar for specific days during your trip time.

Opening Hours:

Shop hours are generally 8 a.m. to 8 p.m., Monday through Saturday. In the summer, many tourist-oriented shops in the Old Town remain open later, even on Sundays. Supermarket hours are often extended.

Banks and post offices: These are usually open from 8 a.m. to 7 p.m. on weekdays and Saturday mornings.

Museums and Attractions: hours vary widely depending on the season. Summer hours are longer, but winter hours may be drastically reduced or even closed. Always check their websites or the Tourist Information Center.

Restaurants: Are often open for lunch (between 12 and 3 p.m.) and supper (6 p.m. to 11 p.m. or later). Cafes stay open all day.

MAINTAINING SAFETY: COMMON SCAMS AND PRECAUTIONS

Trogir is very safe, but like with anywhere, a little vigilance goes a long way.

Pickpocketing: the key item to be aware about, especially in public locations like as the Riva, main square, and markets. Keep valuables safe and out of sight. Do not leave baggage unattended.

Overcharging: Although uncommon, constantly verify your bill in restaurants and bars. If a price appears to be overly exorbitant (for example, a cab without a meter), respectfully inquire about it ahead of time.

ATM skimming: Use ATMs in well-lit, trustworthy places (such as bank branches). Protect your PIN.

"Friendly" Strangers Offering Unsolicited Help or Tours: Be nice, but careful. Follow official guidelines or recommendations from the Tourist Office.

Beach Theft: Avoid leaving valuables unattended on the beach while swimming.

Wrapping Up

Truthfully, common sense is your best protection. Trogir is a delightfully inviting location, and with a little foresight, you may have a terrific and trouble-free day. Now all you have to do is pack your luggage and enjoy yourself!

APPENDIX: TROGIR DIRECTORY.

Keep it handy! It's intended to be a useful resource during your Trogir experience.

RECOMMENDED EATING PLACES: RESTAURANTS, KONOBAS, CAFES

(Price Range Key: € = Budget; €€ = Mid-Range; €€€ = High-End. (These are pretty approximate!)

✓ **Konoba Trs (Old Town**

Vibe: Authentic Dalmatian, gorgeous courtyard, and delicious peka (order ahead!).

Address: Matije Gupca 14, 21220 Trogir.

Phone (roughly): +385 21 881 684.

Price range: €€ - €€

✓ **Restaurant Don Dino (Old Town)**

Vibe: Upscale, modern Croatian/Mediterranean, with a reputation for excellent seafood and presentation.

Address: Ulica Matije Gupca 2, 21220 Trogir.

Phone (approx.): +385 21 882 652.

Price range: €€

✓ **Konoba Škrapa (Čiovo, near the bridge)**

Waterside dining, fresh seafood, and traditional meals are popular among locals and visitors.

Address: Kralja Tomislava 13, 21220 Arbanija (Čiovo).

Phone (roughly): +385 21 888 082.

Price range: €€

✓ **Restaurant Vanjaka (Old Town)**

Vibe: An elegant environment in a historic building, with excellent Dalmatian food.

Address: Radovanov Trg 7, 21220, Trogir

Phone (roughly): +385 21 796 768.

Price range: €€

✓ **Pizzeria Mirkec (Mainland, Near Old Town)**

Vibe: Casual, known for delicious pizza and spaghetti, and typically reasonably priced.

Address: Ulica Kardinala Alojzija Stepinca 10, 21220 Trogir (often part of Guest House Mirkec).

Phone (roughly): +385 21 882 521

Price range: € – €€

✓ **Caffe Bar Smokvica (Riva Old Town)**

Vibe: Excellent place for coffee, beverages, and people-watching on the Riva.

Address: Obala Bana Berislavića 20, 21220, Trogir.

Price range: € for beverages.

✓ Gelateria Bella (Oldtown)

Vibe: Popular for its wonderful ice cream, which comes in a variety of flavors.

Address: Gradska ul. 2, 21220, Trogir (locations change, but there are usually several decent ones!)

Pricing Range: €

ACCOMMODATION LISTINGS: HOTELS, GUESTHOUSES, AND APARTMENTS.

(For a more thorough explanation and applicability, see Chapter 9. Here's a brief reference.)

Brown Beach House & Spa: Put Vlaka 6, Trogir (Čiovo), may be reached at +385 21 355 550.

Hotel Pašike: Sinjska ul. 6, Trogir, +385 21 885 185.

XII Century Heritage Hotel: Ulica Vinka Celija 2, Trogir; +385 21 881 333.

Hostel Trogir: Matije Gupca 10, Trogir. (Check booking sites for contact information.)

ACI Marina Trogir (for boat stays): Put Cumbrijana 22, Trogir; +385 21 881 544

For Apartments/Private Rooms: Use booking.com or Airbnb, or contact the Trogir Tourist Board for advice on local agencies.

MUSEUMS, GALLERIES, AND KEY ATTRACTIONS.

✓ **Saint Lawrence Cathedral (Katedrala Sv. Lovre)**

Address: Trg Ivana Pavla II, Trogir

Opening hours vary by season, although in the summer they are normally 9 a.m. to 6/7 p.m. Check locally.

Website (typically part of the Tourist Board site): tzg-trogir.hr.

✓ **Kamerlengo Fortress**

Address: Obala Bana Berislavića, Trogir.

Opening hours vary, but are longer in the summer (for example, 9 a.m. to 9 p.m.). Check locally.

✓ Trogir Town Museum (Musej Grada Trogira)

Address: Gradska vrata 4, Trogir.

Summer hours are typically 9 a.m. to 1 p.m. and 5 p.m. to 8 p.m., but off-season hours are shorter and closed on Sundays. Check the webpage.

Website address: muzejgradatrogira.hr

- ✓ **Benedictine Monastery of St. Nicholas (Kairos Collection).**

Address: Gradskoga Ul. 35, Trogir.

Opening hours: Limited, usually in the mornings or by appointment. Check with Tourist Information.

- ✓ Krka National Park (Daytrip)

Website (for hours, pricing, and information): np-krka.hr

ESSENTIAL SERVICES

ATMs & Banks (Locations)

ATMs: Available in Old Town (e.g., on Riva, near the main plaza) and mainland Trogir. Search for significant bank logos (PBZ, ZABA, Erste, OTP).

Banks:

Zagrebačka banka (ZABA): Obala kralja Zvonimira, Trogir (Mainland)

Privredna banka Zagreb (PBZ): Ulica kardinala Alojzija Stepinca, Trogir (Mainland):

Other banks also present, especially on the mainland in the market/bus station area.

Pharmacies (Ljekarna) (Locations and Hours)

Ljekarna Trogir (Main Pharmacy): Ulica Blaža Jurjeva Trogiranina, Trogir (Mainland, near market). Open throughout standard hours, with an on-call pharmacist available for emergencies (typically advertised on the door). Smaller branches/private pharmacies may exist in/near Old Town. Look for the green cross.

Hours: Monday through Friday 8 a.m. to 8 p.m., Saturday 8 a.m. to 1/3 p.m.

Medical Clinics & Hospitals (Addresses and Emergency Contacts)

Dom Zdravlja Trogir (Health Center): Ulica kardinala Alojzija Stepinca 17, Trogir (Mainland).

For non-life-threatening conditions, **KBC Split (Clinical Hospital Center Split - Firule or Križine)** is the main hospital in Split for major crises. **Address:** Spinčićeva ul. 1 (Firule) or Šoltanska ul. 1 (Križine), Split. Emergency number: 112.

Police Station (Policija) Address and Contact Details Policijska Postaja Trogir:

Put Muline 1, 21220 Trogir (Mainland).

Emergency Police Number: 192 (or call 112).

Post Offices (Pošta) (Locations)

The main post office is located in Obala kralja Zvonimira in Trogir (near the bridge on the mainland). A smaller branch may be located in the Old Town. Look for the "HP - Hrvatska Pošta" signage.

Parks, Beaches, and Public Spaces (Key Locations).

Riva Promenade: Runs along the southern border of Old Town.

Trg Ivana Pavla II (Main Square): The heart of Old Town.

Okrug Gornji Beach ("Copacabana"): Čiovo Island.

Slatine Beaches: Eastern Čiovo Island.

Pantan Nature Reserve: located east of Trogir on the mainland. Park beside the ancient mill.

Recommended Websites and Emergency Contacts

Trogir Tourist Board: tzg-trogir.hr (Official source of local information).

Croatia National Tourist Board: Croatia.hr (General information about Croatia)

Jadrolinija (ferries): jadrolinija.hr.

Get By Bus (Bus Schedules): getbybus.com.

HAK (Croatian Auto Club, Road Conditions): hak.hr

Emergency number (police, ambulance, and fire): 112

Police: 192.

Ambulance: 194.

Fire Brigade: 193.

Sea Search and Rescue: 195

Roadside Assistance (HAK): 1987.

Wrapping Up

That should offer you a decent toolset of useful information. Trogir is a delightfully manageable town, and with these tips, you'll be ready to explore with confidence. Now go make some amazing memories!

MAP OF TROGIR

https://commons.wikimedia.org/wiki/File:Trogir,_Croatia_OpenStreetMap.png

SCAN IMAGE/
QRCODE
WITH   YOUR
PHONE

TO GET THE
LOCATION IN
REAL TIME

MAP OF THINGS TO DO

https://maps.app.goo.gl/TnX6dMtv8nVQ6uvAA

SCAN IMAGE/
QRCODE
WITH YOUR
PHONE

TO GET THE
LOCATION IN
REAL TIME

MAP OF MUSEUMS

https://maps.app.goo.gl/XBiUSxvvU35P7cY2A

SCAN IMAGE/
QRCODE
WITH YOUR
PHONE

TO GET THE
LOCATION IN
REAL TIME

MAP OF HIKING TRAILS

https://maps.app.goo.gl/bCbmtJG3ZsP7M9UH6

SCAN IMAGE/
QRCODE
WITH YOUR
PHONE

TO GET THE
LOCATION IN
REAL TIME

MAP OF TRANSIT STATIONS

https://maps.app.goo.gl/PPajuKGvd5rfuX467

SCAN IMAGE/
QRCODE
WITH YOUR
PHONE

TO GET THE
LOCATION IN
REAL TIME

MAP OF RESTAURANTS

https://maps.app.goo.gl/EVxbuxCWTfxoQTf7A

SCAN IMAGE/
QRCODE
WITH YOUR
PHONE

TO GET THE
LOCATION IN
REAL TIME